The Liberty That Brings Victory in Christ

Michael Carney

The Liberty That Brings
Victory in Christ

By: Michael Carney

Writings contained herein are by the author unless otherwise stated.

All scriptures are taken from the
King James Bible.

ISBN: 979-8-9872886-2-7

Published By:
Baptist Authors
12400 S Western Ave
Oklahoma City, OK 73170

www.BaptistAuthors.com

PREFACE

The Bible says in Hebrews 12 verses 5 and 6,

> Hebrews 12:5-6 And ye have forgotten the exhortation which speaketh unto you as unto children, My son, despise not thou the chastening of the Lord, nor faint when thou art rebuked of him: 6 For whom the Lord loveth he chasteneth, and scourgeth every son whom he receiveth.

This verse can encourage the reader who knows they are not walking with God or living according to His commands. One might realize that the chastening of the Lord teaches us that we are not right with God, that it matters to us in a personal way that we are not right with God, and that God loves us in a personal and intimate way. The chastening of the Lord may also strengthen our position of eternal security. We know in our heart that God is dealing with us and that reinforces the existence of our personal relationship with God.

This should not try our faith, but strengthen it. It strengthens our faith at a time when our faith is weak. If you see the chastening hand of God it would not cause a man living for God to question the working of God, and a man not living for God may realize where he is at spiritually and discover his need to get right with God. We know, even if we are not willing to admit it, when we are out of fellowship with God.

I believe the trial of our faith comes when we are dealing with the punishing effects of the corruption of sin and we are walking with God, or when we believe we are innocent of sinful deeds yet the results of the sin practiced by others causes problems for us. At one time or another probably every believer has said in their heart, "why does the Lord allow this!" Paul said, "We are troubled on every side yet not distressed; we are perplexed, but not in despair…" (2 Corinthians 4:8). Knowing some of the trials of Paul we should be able to handle our meager trials, but, unfortunately sometimes we do experience the stress and despair.

The question of "why does God allow this or that" is a question people sometimes ask to raise doubts in God, or justify unbelief in the midst of trials and temptations and it can be a tough one. In general we can read what Elihu said to Job and his companions in Job 37:23, "Touching the Almighty, we cannot find him out: he is excellent in power, and in judgment, and in plenty of justice: he will not afflict." Still there are moments when we stress over understanding. Someone else's "why" question plagues our thoughts and may rise to questions in our own heart. The world is full of people who seem to be angry at God and want to express it.

However, as we read in Psalm 2 it is "vain" to "rage" against God. Why would people be so angry at God if God does not exist? I've heard people express rage towards God with a question like, "If God is so good than why did he allow this to happen!" This is followed by the statement expressed in outrage, "that's why I don't believe in God!" Well, I guess you told him, didn't you? It seems to me, that they are expressing anger towards God, not doubt or unbelief in his existence.

If you question, "why does God allow this or why does God do this," you have discerned that something else is in control. If their belief is that God does not exist and that they are the masters of their own destiny, false beliefs and superstitions should not cause them a minute of concern. An expression of outrage towards a being they claim does not exist only supports belief in his existence. If you are making of list of injustices you want to blame him for, wouldn't that mean he held some responsibility for these things? Is not that proof that you believe in God? If God is responsible for the things that affect our lives, doesn't that give Him sovereign authority? Your rage proves your belief in something to rage against.
They "imagine a vain thing." If you are angry at God for his sovereign power, it is vain because if he has sovereign power he has more power than you! What could your anger do but set you against the one in charge? Psalms 2:3 "Let us break their bands asunder, and cast away their cords from us." The cords you seek to loosen, O vain man, is evidence of God's authority.

For the believer, the structure, the authority, and the evidence of

God's power further reinforce our faith in God. The trial comes when we find difficulty in seeing the structure, the authority and the sovereign power of God.

Proverbs 16:4 "The LORD hath made all things for himself: yea, even the wicked for **the day of evil**." Some will struggle with the fact that there is a "day of evil," that God knows it, and that God has a purpose in it. The fact that God made the wicked does not mean that God made them wicked. It only means that God allowed the trial and sees a purpose in the battle. Still there is a struggle to understand why the option even exists.

There is a purpose for the trials of life. James 1:4 "But **let** patience have her perfect work, that ye may be perfect and entire, wanting nothing." Have you ever told someone, "let me finish, before you judge the result." Well, God is still working on us and He knows what He is doing. If we understand that there is a process, a work to be accomplished…perhaps we can relate to the verses before verse 4 and put the whole picture together:

> James 1:2-7 My brethren, count it all joy when ye fall into divers temptations; 3 Knowing *this,* that the trying of your faith worketh patience. 4 But let patience have *her* perfect work, that ye may be perfect and entire, wanting nothing. 5 If any of you lack wisdom, let him ask of God, that giveth to all *men* liberally, and upbraideth not; and it shall be given him. 6 But let him ask in faith, nothing wavering. For he that wavereth is like a wave of the sea driven with the wind and tossed. 7 For let not that man think that he shall receive any thing of the Lord."

The test is the evidence that there is a lesson to be learned and an opportunity to prove it. The test is the opportunity for success, or in academic terms, the test is the opportunity to get a good grade. You are not given a test to fail; you are given a test to demonstrate proficiency in what you learned. The test makes the C student pass and gives glory to the A+.

The, "trying of your faith" is necessary to have patience:

"**PATIENCE**, n. pa'shens. [L. patientia, from patior, to suffer.]

1. The suffering of afflictions, pain, toil, calamity, provocation or other evil, with a calm, unruffled temper; endurance without murmuring or fretfulness..."[1]

Without the trial, we could take patience right out of the dictionary.

.

[1] Webster's 1828 Dictionary, e-Sword version 10.2.0, Copyright © 2000 – 2013.

TABLE OF CONTENTS

THE PRESENCE OF SIN, THE LIBERTY TO LOVE

THE PREMISE OF OUR RELATIONSHIP WITH GOD

The Bible makes several references to the foreknowledge of God. Foreknowledge is defined in Webster's 1828 dictionary, "Knowledge of a thing before it happens; prescience."[2] It is the idea that God knows something before it exists or happens. The word "foreknowledge" in our Bible comes from the Greek word, πρόγνωσις – prognosis.[3] There are several verses that tell us God knew or prognosticated, what would happen before he even began creation:

> Matthew 13:35 That it might be fulfilled which was spoken by the prophet, saying, I will open my mouth in parables; I will utter things which have been kept secret **from the foundation of the world.**

> Hebrews 4:3 For we which have believed do enter into rest, as he said, As I have sworn in my wrath, if they shall enter into my rest: although the works

---

[2] Webster's 1828 Dictionary, e-Sword version 10.2.0, Copyright © 2000 – 2013.

[3] Strong's Greek Lexicon, Online Bible Edition, Version: 4.41, Copyright © 1992 – 2014.

> were finished **from the foundation of the world.**

> Revelation 13:8 And all that dwell upon the earth shall worship him, whose names are not written in the book of life of the Lamb slain **from the foundation of the world.**

For some the foreknowledge of God creates a problem. They question the righteousness of God because of the presence of evil. If God knew that there would be sin, destruction, murder, and sorrow; why did he allow it to take place?

This is where the importance of our liberty comes in. First, let's look at the beginning of sin. The Bible tells us in Romans 5: 12, "Wherefore, as by one man sin entered into the world, and death by sin; and so death passed upon all men, for that all have sinned..." Sin came into the world by the first man, Adam.

The account of how sin was introduced to man is recorded in Genesis:

> Genesis 3:1-10 Now the serpent was more subtil than any beast of the field which the LORD God had made. And he said unto the woman, Yea, hath God said, Ye shall not eat of every tree of the garden? 2 And the woman said unto the serpent, We may eat of the fruit of the trees of the garden: 3 But of the fruit of the tree which *is* in the midst of the garden, God hath said, Ye shall not eat of it, neither shall ye touch it, lest ye die. 4 And the serpent said unto the woman, Ye shall not surely die: 5 For God doth know that in the day ye eat thereof, then your eyes shall be opened, and ye shall be as gods, knowing good and evil. 6 And when the woman saw that the tree *was* good for food, and that it *was* pleasant to the eyes, and a tree to be desired to make *one* wise, she took of the fruit thereof, and did eat, and gave also unto her

> husband with her; **and he did eat.** 7 And the eyes
> of them both were opened, and they knew that they
> *were* naked; and they sewed fig leaves together, and
> made themselves aprons. 8 And they heard the
> voice of the LORD God walking in the garden in
> the cool of the day: and Adam and his wife hid
> themselves from the presence of the LORD God
> amongst the trees of the garden. 9 And the LORD
> God **called unto Adam**, and said unto him, Where
> *art* thou? 10 And he said, I heard thy voice in the
> garden, and I was afraid, because I *was* naked; and I
> hid myself.

Eve was tempted to sin, but Adam sinned willingly and began the sinful nature in man and the result of sin. So, begins the reign of death. Adam and Eve are cast out of the garden. Creation is changed. Soon, they bear children; first Cain and then Abel. Our first parents experience one of the greatest tragedies. Cain, the first man born in this world, murders his brother Abel. This is the history of the first family.

Here is where questions begin and the trial of faith starts. "WHAT! God knew us from 'the foundation of the world' and he let it continue? Why didn't he stop the devil? Why didn't he stop Cain?"

Throughout the writings of the Bible we find many instances where evil causes sorrow and grief to man. Wicked people, wicked kingdoms, and injustice against those who are innocent will be found in the Biblical history of men, the Jews, and the church.

We can go back even further to look at the origin of sin…The Bible teaches us how the devil came into being:

> Isaiah 14:12-15 How art thou fallen from heaven,
> O Lucifer, son of the morning! *how* art thou cut
> down to the ground, which didst weaken the
> nations! 13 For thou hast said in thine heart, I will
> ascend into heaven, I will exalt my throne above the
> stars of God: I will sit also upon the mount of the
> congregation, in the sides of the north: 14 I will
> ascend above the heights of the clouds; I will be like

> the most High. 15 Yet thou shalt be brought down to hell, to the sides of the pit.

God created all things and knew that Satan would fall and tempt man. He knew that man would sin and take on a sinful nature. He knew that sin would cost the price of the precious blood of the Savior **"BEFORE THE FOUNDATION OF THE WORLD!"**

Does God have evil intentions? Is He a God of hate? Does he love us? He does not have evil intentions, He is not a God of hate, and YES He does love us! In fact, His love is the reason God allowed the fall of man and does not control our every step or our every thought.

When God created man He gave him the capacity to have emotions and established an emotional connection between each other and between us and him. God did not make us as some man might make a tire on an assembly line. Once the tire is made, he hopes he did the best job he could, but he sends it on down the road. God wanted us to have an intimate personal relationship with Him. He wanted the relationship to continue and develop our whole life and with each man that was born. God did not decide to have maker product relationship with men. God determined that the relationship with man would be based on love. He would love us, and by love we would honor and glorify Him.
He expresses this connection in the creation and plans for the nation of Israel.

> Deuteronomy 7:6-7 For thou *art* an holy people unto the LORD thy God: the LORD thy God hath chosen thee to be a special people unto himself, above all people that *are* upon the face of the earth. 7 The LORD did not set **his love** upon you, nor choose you, because ye were more in number than any people; for ye *were* the fewest of all people…

God made us to be like Him and to fellowship with Him and, "God is love." 1 John 4:8. If God is love, what other means can he determine our relationship to be established upon? If God is love,

He cannot help but express love and love has its own defining characteristics and necessities for existence. If we can understand that the trying of our faith works patience, we might realize there is something that "works" love. One thing is certain, when you have a relationship with God, love is necessary.

LOVE is of highest importance in the life of a believer.

- Love is a command:

  John 13:34 A new commandment I give unto you, That ye love one another; as I have loved you, that ye also love one another.
- Love is a gift

  1 Corinthians 13:13 And now abideth faith, hope, charity, these three; but the greatest of these *is* charity.
- Love is a fruit of the Spirit

  Galatians 5:22 But the fruit of the Spirit is love, joy, peace, longsuffering, gentleness, goodness, faith,…
- Love should be part of our testimony

  Ephesians 5:2 And walk in love, as Christ also hath loved us, and hath given himself for us an offering and a sacrifice to God for a sweetsmelling savour.

Love is the basis of our relationship with God and the evidence of our relationship with God. As it was with God's plan and provision for salvation, God also planned our relationship with him to be based on love.

> Ephesians 1:4 According as he hath chosen us in him **before the foundation of the world**, that we should be holy and without blame before him **in love…**

THE EVIDENCE OF GOD'S LOVE

The fruit of the Spirit in the life of a believer is the evidence that the person is walking under the Spirit's control. Love is not without evidence. There is a difference between a relationship that is based on love and a relationship that is based on circumstances of authority.

When I was young I was in junior navy program called, "Sea Cadets." We observed the same rank and authority as the regular navy. One time I was staying on the base for the weekend and I walked from the barracks to the mess hall. I was wearing my dress white uniform, which, from a distance looked exactly like the regular navy uniform. While I was walking an Admiral visiting the base was being driven down the street in a jeep. I saw the jeep, and the officer sitting in it, but did not think about the proper response. As a typical teenager, I took a good long look at the gold braids on the Admiral's uniform. The driver hit the brakes stood, yelling something, and demanded I show respect. I immediately snapped to attention and saluted, and I held that salute until one was returned and the jeep continued on its way. Now, I couldn't hear all the conversation that took place between the petty officer and the Admiral, but I feel pretty certain he did not say, "look how he loves me!" Let's face it, I don't know what they would have done but I was scared to attention!

You cannot believe that a decision made by demand or force could compare to a relationship of love. Love must be given by choice. The element of free will is essential for love to exist.

Since God wanted to establish a relationship of love, the evidence of that relationship must be liberty. There has to be a freedom to love or not to love, or else there is no love. Imagine if we had no choice but to live a holy life; if the devil was immediately destroyed and no temptation ever took place. That sounds great, but there would be no volition, no free choice to love. Everyone would love God and there would be no option. Is that really love?

In order for love to exist a person must have a choice. They must have the freedom to walk away or choose love. God did not want eternal automatons. I was thinking about this point and I took the opportunity to search the internet about God's love for men and the need to choose love in order for love to exist. I was surprised to find as much information as did. Not just on God's love in general, but on many articles and YouTube messages on the fact that love can only exist on a platform of free choice.

It seems like a simple response to a question that is often asked, "if God loves us, why does he allow_______." Some people will not except there must be free choice. They seem to believe that God exists to take care of every need of man and if He does not, He is not a God of love. God does not exist to meet all our wants and desires or resolve every conflict or need. You having the things you want in this world is not His sole purpose for existing nor is a demand or expectation to get everything you want a basis for a loving relationship. God will not be a slave to your will, and He will not base His love for you on you being a slave for Him. God's decision to love us, and your decision, your choice to love God is necessary for the liberty to love to exist.

God has chosen to establish a relationship with us based on love. Love is often shown at the expense of the person expressing that love. God loves us and died for us on the cross. It was His choice and that is love. In fact, it was his choice to love because of our sinful condition and because we needed His love. God was free to provide salvation, as He was the only one that could, but he was also free to deny it. I think this is something people don't understand. He chose to prove how great His love was for us by sacrificing his only begotten Son on the cross for our sins.

> Romans 5:8 But God commendeth his love toward us, in that, while we were yet sinners, Christ died for us.

We love God and show Him respect and honor. We may choose to obey the Word rather than the flesh, though we really want to obey the flesh. This is love. We choose God. However, if there were no choice there would be no love. Love is part of a system of choices. We also have to know what to reject to show love. We see someone who is mean spirited or evil and we recognize evil as the choice that is contrary to love. WE choose not to show evil. Perhaps someone acts towards us in an evil way; we see retaliation as not having love. This was the example of Christ on the cross..."Father, forgive them..."

If there was no free will, love would not exist. If we must be able to choose love, we must be able to choose not to love. A place of no love is a dark place and a place that will not be in fellowship with light. But, that place must exist in order for the choice to be made. We may think that love can't exist unless evil is stopped. Well, we may not think that every single evil thing must be stopped, but the worst evil should not be allowed. Or at least the evil thing that changed the course of our life, took our loved one, or injured us in some way must be stopped.

However, if every evil act was not stopped, then there would be condemnation for every evil act that was permitted. If God stopped one person from being harmed, he would have to stop every person and every act of harm or someone would not believe they were loved. There would be an endless connection between one event and another from day to day. If God were to stop a murder, should he stop a sickness? If a sickness, should he stop a broken bone? If a broken bone, should he stop a sprain? When there are no more broken bones a sprain would be major and when all sprains are gone how could we tolerate a bruise? Without transgressions, without sin, there would be no freedom. The fundamental relationship between God and man would be completely changed. Man would have no choice but to honor and obey God, love would be irrelevant.

When sin entered the world the choice between sin and holiness was created. For some, the opportunity to sin becomes a failure, to others it is part of a victorious testimony that honors and glorifies God. We witness this choice in the life of Joseph:

> Genesis 39:7-9 And it came to pass after these things, that his master's wife cast her eyes upon Joseph; and she said, Lie with me. 8 But he refused, and said unto his master's wife, Behold, my master wotteth not what *is* with me in the house, and he hath committed all that he hath to my hand; 9 *There is* none greater in this house than I; neither hath he kept back any thing from me but thee, because thou *art* his wife: how then can I do this great wickedness, **and sin against God**?

If the question was asked, who did Joseph love more, or rather, what did Joseph love more, to fulfill his own lusts or be faithful to God? The answer is clear. Joseph respected his master, but he was faithful to God. But for the choice, the act of love would not have been expressed. The test was necessary for the decision. At that moment Joseph pays a heavy price for his love for God. Yet, it does not deter his love for God. He continues to live the testimony of a believer.

> Genesis 39:20 And Joseph's master took him, and put him into the prison, a place where the king's prisoners *were* bound: and he was there in the prison.

> Genesis 39:23 The keeper of the prison looked not to any thing *that was* under his hand; because the LORD was with him, and *that* which he did, the LORD made *it* to prosper.

Joseph continued to love God and carry the testimony of his faith in him. In the end we find out that prison was actually the best place for Joseph. From prison Joseph is elevated to the greatest position in his life. Prison was the opportunity for the baker and the butler to share their dreams with Joseph. As an innocent man, one may sit in prison and accuse God of his lack of love or mercy, but we learn sometimes where we think we should be and where we need to be is not the same place. The God of love knew this.

Some may believe that it would have been better for Joseph to be at home with his coat of many colors. But, through a series of choices there was a path paved that lead Joseph to the highest position in the world.

> Genesis 41:56-57 And the famine was over all the face of the earth: And Joseph opened all the storehouses, and sold unto the Egyptians; and the famine waxed sore in the land of Egypt. 57 And all countries came into Egypt to Joseph for to buy *corn;* because that the famine was *so* sore in all lands.

Joseph had a choice of faith and of doubt. He had a choice of sin and of righteousness. He had a choice of anger, resentment, bitterness, hate, or love. He chose love. We can see that choice and we know that that choice brought honor to God. God was glorified in his decision to love God and in his decision to forgive his brothers. If there was no choice…everything would have been different. Without that choice there would be no love.

Those who were against Joseph expressed envy, lusts, and jealousy. In their sin they meant to exact revenge and sorrow based purely on their envy of Joseph's success. But, God used their sinful plots to create His plan. It also gave Joseph a position above all the others in the site of God; a man who would choose God and not the flesh. Their very defeat was his victory. The presence of sin gave the liberty to love.

LOVE IS NOT WITHOUT RESPONSIBILITY

Freedom of will does not negate responsibility. Because man has the freedom to choose whether to do right or wrong does not make his creator the one that caused him to make the decision. Love has provided choices; some have made many bad choices. God is not responsible for the decisions that people make to reject his kindness and love. He is not responsible for the wickedness that we decide to do.

> Genesis 4:4-5 And Abel, he also brought of the firstlings of his flock and of the fat thereof. And the LORD had respect unto Abel and to his offering: 5 But unto Cain and to his offering he had not respect. And Cain was very wroth, and his countenance fell.

> Genesis 4:8 And Cain talked with Abel his brother: and it came to pass, when they were in the field, that Cain rose up against Abel his brother, and slew him.

> 1 John 3:12 Not as Cain, *who* was of that wicked one, and slew his brother. And wherefore slew he him? Because his own works were evil, and his brother's righteous.

Cain rose up and killed Abel. God allowed it to happen, but God does not shoulder the responsibility for Cain's anger and murder. Abel knew the offering that God would accept.

> Hebrews 11:4 By faith Abel offered unto God a more excellent sacrifice than Cain, by which he obtained witness that he was righteous, God testifying of his gifts: and by it he being dead yet speaketh.

This truth was taught to Abel either by his parents or by God himself, but somehow the significance of that sacrifice was known. Abel offered an offering because of faith, apparently, because of the faith he had in what the offering meant. Abel's sacrifice was not a witness that he was a shepherd. It was a witness that he was righteous. Righteousness comes by faith; faith in God and his propitiation for our sin. If Abel had access to this truth his older brother would have as well. God's response to Cain's anger reveals His displeasure with Cain's choice of offerings:

> Genesis 4:6-7 And the LORD said unto Cain, Why art thou wroth? and why is thy countenance fallen? 7 If thou doest well, shalt thou not be accepted? and if thou doest not well, sin lieth at the door. And unto thee *shall be* his desire, and thou shalt rule over him.

The liberty to sin does not remove the responsibility of the sinner. Nor, does it remove the results of sin. A garden of sin is what you have planted. A garden of sin is what you will care for. A garden of sin is where you will gather the fruits of your labor. God made it clear from the beginning that sin had consequences.

> Genesis 2:17 But of the tree of the knowledge of good and evil, thou shalt not eat of it: for in the day that thou eatest thereof thou shalt surely die.

God allowed sin to come, but he did so with a warning of the results of sin.

> Genesis 3:21 Unto Adam also and to his wife did the LORD God make coats of skins, and clothed them.

Sin brought death and death brought sacrifice. In order to have love, we were given free will. Free will meant we had to be given the choice to obey the commandments of God or pursue our other love, the lust of our flesh. Because we had free will we chose the lusts of the flesh over the love of God and have continued to do so:

> John 3:19 And this is the condemnation, that light is come into the world, and men loved darkness rather than light, because their deeds were evil.

Love went one more step and established reconciliation. The ultimate sacrifice for love was the cost of redemption.

> Revelation 13:8 And all that dwell upon the earth shall worship him, whose names are not written in the book of life of the Lamb slain from the foundation of the world.

God does not shoulder the responsibility of sin, but because of love, he shouldered the payment for sin. Our responsibility is to place our faith in His payment. It is to receive this gift of salvation provided by the love of God. Sin also provided the opportunity for God to show the ultimate sacrifice. It gave him the opportunity to have sacrificial love. It is not that God wanted us to sin, but that he was willing to pay the price for free will.

A LOVING RELATIONSHIP IS NOT A WEAK UNDEFINED RELATIONSHIP

Sometimes people use love as a reason to not confront someone who might be in sin or spiritual danger. You may have heard someone say, "I just love everyone…" It is a great sentiment and one that should apply to believers on some level, but if it is an answer to why we do not define boundaries in our relationships and stand for what is right it is not a Biblical type of love.

I have four children and I love each one of them. As a dad you enjoy that moment when one of your children is excited and happy about some good thing you did for them or gave them. But, it is not a license or "love" to give them everything they may want.

I have a gluten allergy, but before I did one of my favorite things was Oreo cookies. When we were missionaries sometime around 2000 – 2001, a church in Mississippi sent me a whole case of Oreo cookies! That's twelve packages! We ate the whole thing in about six weeks. When I say, "we" I got more than my fair share. However, we all had some. I remember my oldest son loved the cookies. I know if I had decided to give him Oreos three times a day, every day, until his teeth fell out he would have been happy. I would have enjoyed his joy and I'm sure his eyes would have lit up every time I came from the pantry.

Although, we want that kind of joy and reception; it is not a good thing if it is destructive to the party we love. My response of giving him more cookies than he should have would only be a reaction to his joy in me giving him what he would want. I would be responding to his pleasure in my actions, but not to the responsibility I should shoulder as a parent. It would feel good to me to see his happiness, but it would not be good for him. That would be selfish on my part. We make our children eat a balanced meal because of love. We do not deny them the desires of their heart, or their belly, because we do not love them. We have a more mature understanding of what is healthy and why it is important. It would be easier not to deny them things they desire, especially if it elicits a mournful response. However, with their best interest at heart, despite their pleas to the opposite, we moderate their desserts. At the moment it is not a pleasant thing to deny people we love, but because of love it is necessary. Love is not weak.

> 1 Peter 1:22 Seeing ye have purified your souls in obeying the truth through the Spirit unto unfeigned love of the brethren, *see that ye* love one another with a pure heart fervently:...

Love must be pure, love cannot be an excuse for corruption, it cannot be an excuse for sin, and it cannot be an excuse for lusts. It must remain pure to the one who gives love, to the one who receives love and to the one who has given the real example of love. I've heard people say, "Tough love." It's really not tough love, it's just love. Love is pure and sometimes pure is hard to take, but it is only love when it is pure.

> Romans 12:9 *Let* love be without dissimulation. Abhor that which is evil; cleave to that which is good.

Love should not be hypocritical; the constant guide of love is purity. It is not love to excuse that which is evil and to cleave to that which is bad. It is love to "*abhor that which is evil*" and *"cleave to that which good…" (Romans 12:9)* because you care about the influence or impact evil and good have on people you love and people you influence. If you truly love others you will not accept behavior that is destructive.

You will desire and use whatever influence you have to put them right.

> Ephesians 4:15 But speaking the truth in love, may grow up into him in all things, which is the head, *even* Christ:

Truth is an important part of love. Some people treat the matter of truth as if it were a gray area. The world has a difficult time with absolutes because they cannot agree on a foundation of authority. But our foundation of authority is the Word of God and it defines truth.

Truth is emphasized in the Word of God and it should be in our hearts and in our actions towards others. Philippians 4:8 defines what is good to keep in our heart. I was thinking it is also a good test to see if God's will is being accomplished in our decisions. The will of God for us is something we should be able to entertain in our hearts.

> Philippians 4:8 Finally, brethren, whatsoever things are true, whatsoever things *are* honest, whatsoever things *are* just, whatsoever things *are* pure, whatsoever things *are* lovely, whatsoever things *are* of good report; if *there be* any virtue, and if *there be* any praise, think on these things.

- True - is it defended or taught by principle or command by God's Word. Is it true to the Bible and our Lord?

- Honest - do we have to embellish it when we tell others? Are there several versions according to who we are talking to? Are you being honest with yourself, or do you have to make excuses to counter convictions you have?

- Just - is it just towards God and men? Does it cause us to honor God as we should in our testimony and doctrine? Is it fair in respect to our authority, church, friends, family, and to those we may have pecuniary obligations? In respect to how it affects others, would we want the same treatment?

- Pure - does it stand on its own merit without exception or need for explanation or excuse? Is what we have in our heart about it godly? Can others of like faith see the obvious good? Can it stand on its own in the light? Does it bother us to evaluate it?

- Lovely - does it encourage love toward others? Does it promote brotherly love?

- Good report - is it good to tell others? Does it glorify The Lord in testimony?

- Virtue - does doing it or making this decision demonstrate our obedience to God?

- Praise - can godly people praise our decisions and actions as blessings from God? Would we rejoice for others if they make the same plan or decisions? Is this something that would cause others to say, "Praise the Lord, someone did this?"

Love will always try to correct wrongs, protect the innocent or ignorant, it will always try to mend and forgive, and when necessary chasten and judge. Love is guided by faith in the truth. Love considers the outcome of your actions, the affect and the result it will have on others. Love is worthy of everything we should think upon. Love can only exist by choice. Freedom makes love work.

Yes, God allowed sin to exist and he paid the price to redeem us from the penalty of it. God established a relationship with us that would require love and love has its boundaries and costs. It is not weak, it is strong and it has a testimony of everything that is good. Sin is not our final demise. Sin has given us the opportunity of choice and of free will. It has given us the liberty to love and has proven God's deep and unmeasurable love for us.

THE BATTLE OF SIN, OUR LIBERTY TO HAVE VICTORY

THERE WILL BE A BATTLE

History can be inspirational. I've always enjoyed it. I remember in Jr. High I had a history teacher who was not very popular. She was academic, a bit difficult, and somewhat of a curmudgeon. Most of the kids I knew did not like her and made fun of her behind her back. At that carnal time of my youth, I was just trying to fit in. I didn't say anything, maybe laughed at the jokes, but secretly I loved the class and looked forward to it every day. During that time we were studying the American Civil War. I do not remember much about Jr. High School, but there were things said in that class that I think about still.

My interest in history has caused me to watch many documentaries and read many articles and books on history. As I acquired information one of my favorite sources became firsthand accounts of history, or "primary sources." We tend to look at history as a whole. We fought this battle and won! Yay for us! However primary sources will reveal the intimate pain and misery of the battle. The fears and prejudices of the participants in the record rise to the surface. People suffered to win a conflict, settle a land, or establish a nation. Throughout recorded history there have been many heroes. I have realized, no matter what side you are on or where in the world you are there is always one thing that is necessary to have a victory – a battle.

You cannot have a hero without a fight and you cannot have a victory without a battle.

> 1 John 5:4 For whatsoever is born of God overcometh the world: and this is the victory that overcometh the world, *even* our faith.

We love to sing of victory and we love to hear messages about the victorious Christian life, but we don't want the battle. You cannot have one without the other! Do you want to have a victory? You must have a battle. The greater the battle the greater the victory:

> 1 Corinthians 15:54 So when this corruptible shall have put on incorruption, and this mortal shall have put on immortality, then shall be brought to pass the saying that is written, Death is swallowed up in victory. But thanks *be* to God, which giveth us the victory through our Lord Jesus Christ.

We rejoice in the victory of our Lord over death, but that victory came through suffering and sacrifice.

> Mark 10:34 And they shall mock him, and shall scourge him, and shall spit upon him, and shall kill him: and the third day he shall rise again.

The Lord not only expected a battle, He knew the intimate details. The battle was prophesied about a thousand years before it took place:

> Psalms 22:7-8 All they that see me laugh me to scorn: they shoot out the lip, they shake the head, *saying,* 8 He trusted on the LORD *that* he would deliver him: let him deliver him, seeing he delighted in him.

> [Matthew 27:41-43 Likewise also the chief priests mocking *him,* with the scribes and elders, said, 42 He saved others; himself he cannot save. If he be the King of Israel, let him now come down

> from the cross, and we will believe him. 43 He trusted in God; let him deliver him now, if he will have him: for he said, I am the Son of God.]
>
> 16 For dogs have compassed me: the assembly of the wicked have inclosed me: they pierced my hands and my feet.
>
> 18 They part my garments among them, and cast lots upon my vesture.
>
> [Matthew 27:35 And they crucified him, and parted his garments, casting lots: that it might be fulfilled which was spoken by the prophet, They parted my garments among them, and upon my vesture did they cast lots.]

Our Lord knew what would happen and in an amazing show of God's sovereignty even the enemies of Christ could not help but do what the scripture said they would do. What an amazing prophecy!

As the Lord hung there in pain, beaten, spit upon, mocked, and humiliated the scribes, priests, and elders looked on and participated in the horror of the three hours of darkness. I could imagine they believed themselves to be victorious. I could believe they were ready to clap their hands and say, "we won!" But as a hint of the power of the victor that hung before them, suddenly there was a cry from the cross. One of the last things our Lord spoke was to quote the first verse of the Psalm that prophesied the day:

> Psalms 22:1 My God, my God, why hast thou forsaken me?

What shudder went through the bones of the scribe that thought to himself, "that sounds familiar," and then to look at the scene before him and realize, "I'm the dog!" "This is Psalm 22!"

What carried the Lord through the battle was the victory. As certain as He knew the pain, He knew the victory that would follow:

> Hebrews 12:2 Looking unto Jesus the author and finisher of *our* faith; who **for the joy** that was set before him endured the cross, despising the shame, and is set down at the right hand of the throne of God.

I recently heard a statement from an unbeliever who suggested a moral accusation could be made against God because he allowed His "child" to die on the cross. God did not allow Christ to die on the cross for the sake of suffering. Christ died on the cross for the victory! He gave His life and died in order to conquer death! He and He alone could live the life that could be sacrificed for this purpose with the result of victory. Death could not be conquered without His death.

Why do I struggle so? Why all the battles before us? How come we can't just get a break! Because, dear Christian, as with our Lord and Saviour, God wants us to have a victory therefore we must have a battle. The battle is for the victory. The battle is the fuel with which the glorious flames of victory burn.

The Lord lived the example of enduring the battle and gaining the victory.

> 1 Peter 2:19-25 For this *is* thankworthy, if a man
> for conscience toward God endure grief, suffering
> wrongfully. 20 For what glory *is it,* if, when ye be
> buffeted for your faults, ye shall take it patiently?
> but if, when ye do well, and suffer *for it,* ye take it
> patiently, this *is* acceptable with God. 21 For even
> hereunto were ye called: because Christ also
> suffered for us, leaving us an example, that ye
> should follow his steps: 22 Who did no sin,
> neither was guile found in his mouth: 23 Who,
> when he was reviled, reviled not again; when he
> suffered, he threatened not; but committed *himself*
> to him that judgeth righteously: 24 Who his own
> self bare our sins in his own body on the tree, that
> we, being dead to sins, should live unto

> righteousness: by whose stripes ye were healed. 25 For ye were as sheep going astray; but are now returned unto the Shepherd and Bishop of your souls.

Why were we given this example of suffering? It was not for us to live a life of woe and pain, or asceticism. It was for us to fight the battle and gain the victory. Yes, the Lord suffered greatly and gave himself on the cross where he *"tasted death for every man…" (Hebrews 2:9).* But, in doing so He also saw a marvelous victory, <u>**the resurrection**</u>. In order for Christ to have the resurrection there had to be death. He had to die. <u>The battle was for the victory</u>.

THE VICTORY IS CERTAIN!

Some people believe in the battle, but do not believe in the victory. From time to time I meet believers who are hopeless and defeated in heart concerning the battles we fight. Time and turmoil has worn them down and they have arrived at the conclusion that things will not get better. Galatians 6:9 says, "And let us not be weary in well doing: for in due season we shall reap, if we faint not." There are two phrases that stand out to me. One is "well doing." This is talking about doing things that are good. One of the things that Philippians 4:8 tells us to think about are things that, "are of good report." Good things you would do are things that would make up a good report; things that would be good to others and good to God. If we grow tired of doing well, we are not focusing on right and wrong and what is pleasing to the Lord; we are focusing on what we believe should be the outcome. We are having a problem with our expectations. Regardless of whether or not we ever see the harvest, we need to commit to doing what is good.

The second phrase is "due season." If you take some time and study this phrase out you will find that it is not just talking about a right time or the right season, it is really saying the season or time that is right for you. God is not suggesting you wait for the sake of waiting, although there is a lesson to be learned in waiting, but He is talking about a plan He may be bringing together especially for you.

As a youth in Boston I remember standing on the street in 1969. My siblings and some of the neighbor kids were talking about the upcoming Apollo 11 mission. We were going to the moon and the space age was in full swing! I remember we fantasized that by the time I would graduate high school in 1980 we would be flying all over the solar system. By 2000, when I would be 38, which was older than my parents at the time, we would be living like the "Jetsons" with moving sidewalks, flying saucers for cars, meals in a pill, and a dog named Astro! Yeah, we were pretty far off there. We also imagined what life would be like, how many children we might have, and what kind of career we might pursue.

I realized by 1980 I was not going to be financing a flying saucer anytime soon, but I also had life plans that would not materialize the way I thought. After college I served the Lord in my local church, and then I had opportunities to serve Him in other churches. I thought it would be good if I married, had children, and continued in the work I imagined would be best for me. God had different designs. I see that now, but in life sometimes I wrestled with God's plans. I was frustrated with God's plans and maybe even complained about them. In 1992 at the age of 29 I resolved that I could be happy being in whatever state God would have me to live. When I say, "I resolved that" I don't mean it like we sometimes mean it when we claim that we will accept God's will, secretly hoping His will agreed with our desire. I was single and had come to the resolve that if God wanted me to be single for my whole life, I would know it was His plan, His will, and the best thing for me. It was a moment of surrender.

In January 1993 I met my wife Lynne. I first saw her on my first Sunday morning service at the Lighthouse Children's Home in Kosciusko, MS. She was working as a helper in the school and also lived in the dorm with the girls. I arrived at 1:00 AM on January 17, 1993. I went to bed a few hours and got up to go to church. That morning, as I walked in to the cafeteria/chapel, I saw her reading her Bible at the one of the tables. I looked at her for just a few seconds, but it seemed much longer. At that moment I had peace in my heart that she was the woman for me and that God would give her to me for a wife. I did not know how it would happen, but I was right. We met in January, wed in September, surrendered to the mission field one year later in September of 1994, and arrived in Hungary September of 1995. What that was, was God's "due season" for me.

It may not ever be the plan for anyone else, but for me, God knew my plans much better than I could fanaticize on a sidewalk in Boston at the age of 7. I could have never planned or imagined the wonderful plan God had for my life and the opportunities and joy it would bring. Galatians 6:9 is not about evaluating God's plan or even imagining what God's plan is, it is understanding that the plan concerning our life is known by the Lord and will be the best plan for us. To forsake the path that will lead us to His plan will be to forsake the victorious life He wants us to have.

IF YOU ARE LOOKING FOR A REASON NOT TO EXPECT VICTORY, SOMEONE WILL BE HAPPY TO GIVE IT!

Despite what some may believe criticism and complaining are not spiritual gifts. Neither is that sense of reality that helps you to understand that "you are not going to win them all," and "don't give yourself false hopes" or high expectations. If you are open to it, there are many people who are willing to list your failing credentials and bring down any hope you may have of living in victory. People are always willing to give someone what they may call, "a healthy dose of reality." There are times when the reality is more obvious to others than it is to us. But when it comes to spiritual trust and the work that God can do, anything short of trusting in Him fails to place hope in the right person. *Proverbs 24:10 "If thou faint in the day of adversity, thy strength is small."* I don't think this verse is given to kick you when you are down. I think it points out that our source of strength might be misplaced. If you faint in the day of adversity and your strength was small, maybe you were not supposed to be facing the adversity in your strength. Maybe, you should have been strengthened by the LORD.

We are living in a time when people have resolved themselves that they can't win the battle over sin. Christians believe unbelievers cannot repent of sin, overcome sin, and live a victorious life for God. Many times I've felt that people were being dealt with as if the person they are, (defeated, in spiritual bondage, or lost,) is a person they

always will be. The kid we bring on the van who has the broken home is somehow beyond the expectation of the victorious Christian life. The heroin addict that hears the gospel will always be some kind of lesser Christian that is off and on again in his faithfulness. The immoral young person that made a mistake is just that kind of person and we can only hope they don't make that mistake again. The apathetic teenager living for his lusts is just that way these days, as if a generation of teachers and parents have decided the battle is to loose! Victory is only for those who have little battles. The kind of battles we all know we can win. -- This is not true!
When people say things like, "well, we won't see any more revivals like that!" Or, "things aren't like they use to be, it's much harder now!" Essentially, we are hearing justification to lower our expectations concerning the work of God in our lives and the lives of those we know. If it was only applied to the notion of a world-wide revival and that we believe that won't happen because we live in the last days, I can understand. I understand that 2 Timothy 3:1 tells us, *"in the last days perilous times shall come."* I understand that verse 13 says, *"…evil men and seducers shall wax worse and worse, deceiving, and being deceived."* As it is evident that we are getting closer to the time when our Lord will return, we may not expect all evil men to disappear and all apostasy to stop. However the next verse tells us, *"But continue thou in the things which thou hast learned and hast been assured of…"*

Okay Paul, you want the preacher to continue. Continue in what? 2 Timothy 4:2, *"Preach the word; be instant in season, out of season; reprove, rebuke, exhort with all longsuffering and doctrine."*

We are not instructed by God during the last days to give up. We are not to anticipate a time when we will not pray or believe in the power of God. We must reach out to those who will hear the message with the truth. I believe Paul believed the Lord would return in his lifetime. As the time of his departure from this world was at hand, I believe since he now saw that the Lord would not return in his life, he believed He would most certainly return in Timothy's. Consider the work that Timothy was doing during this time, and the work Paul was charging him to continue. There wasn't any indication that Paul anticipated a lessoning of the work of God.

All indications were that he and the believers at this time, with much persecution, planned to reach the uttermost parts of the earth and preach until the day Jesus came. There was no break in the expectations of what God could do in a church or in the life of a believer. They fully expected the battle to be more difficult and for opposition to grow, but they were resolved that God would continue to work. 2 Timothy 4:5 *"But watch thou in all things, endure afflictions, do the work of an evangelist, make full proof of thy ministry."*

It is true; people have heard the message in more places today than in years ago. In my youth, I never heard the term, "born again." Today it is difficult to find someone who hasn't. It is harder to find people that are open to the message, though there are many who have not heard the message in a Biblical context. There is a spark of interest one sees when a person hears something for the very first time and that may be less likely to find in many places. It may be we have to dig the well a little bit deeper to hit water, but it doesn't mean we should stop digging. We should count ourselves worthy to be chosen by God to stand in these days as Mordecai charged Esther concerning the cause of the Jews:

> Esther 4:14 For if thou altogether holdest thy peace at this time, *then* shall there enlargement and deliverance arise to the Jews from another place; but thou and thy father's house shall be destroyed: and who knoweth whether thou art come to the kingdom for *such* a time as this?

The heat of the battle is not a cause to give up. If the commander calls for us to continue, we can trust He knows the enemy and the battle set before us. We must be faithful for every last soul:

> 2 Kings 19:3-4 And they said unto him, Thus saith Hezekiah, This day *is* a day of trouble, and of rebuke, and blasphemy: for the children are come to the birth, and *there is* not strength to bring forth. 4 It may be the LORD thy God will hear all the words of Rabshakeh, whom the king of Assyria his master hath sent to reproach the living God; and will reprove the words which the LORD thy

> God hath heard: wherefore lift up *thy* prayer for the remnant that are left.

We may be in a time when we do not expect to find as many opportunities to present the gospel to someone who has never heard it before. Some will press on knowing the work is hard, witnessing to all they can, but expecting few to respond. It is a difficult time, in some places more than others.

However knowing the promises and power of God we should never expect that God cannot work in the hearts of His children. To see the world as difficult waters to fish in is one thing, but to believe God will stop working on the ones already caught is another. Some dismiss the idea that God can give believers a victorious life. So much so, that people readily except ungodliness in our churches and personal defeat with sin as if it MUST BE. You can find believers who will expect to be in bondage to sin or expect other believers in church to be in bondage to fleshly lusts. They literally believe you cannot stop the lust of the flesh or expect God's people to live godly lives, so accept it. Well, I don't accept it! I do believe people can have victory. I do not accept people the way they are, because I know God is a God who can change people and make them what they cannot be without Christ. I believe in victory, but not because it is what I hope, but rather because we have the promises of God's Word:

> 1 Peter 5:6-9 Humble yourselves therefore under the mighty hand of God, that he may exalt you in due time: 7 Casting all your care upon him; for he careth for you. 8 Be sober, be vigilant; because your adversary the devil, as a roaring lion, walketh about, seeking whom he may devour: 9 Whom resist stedfast in the faith, knowing that the same afflictions are accomplished in your brethren that are in the world.

> James 4:6-10 But he giveth more grace. Wherefore he saith, God resisteth the proud, but giveth grace unto the humble. 7 Submit yourselves therefore to

> God. Resist the devil, and he will flee from you. 8 Draw nigh to God, and he will draw nigh to you. Cleanse *your* hands, *ye* sinners; and purify *your* hearts, *ye* double minded. 9 Be afflicted, and mourn, and weep: let your laughter be turned to mourning, and *your* joy to heaviness. 10 Humble yourselves in the sight of the Lord, and he shall lift you up.

It is the enemy that will try to convince people that there is no reason to even try. Any enemy would love the opposing army to lay down their weapons and win the victory with little or no effort. For some believers the victory is given to the enemy by default because, there is a battle. I do not know if we will revive our country or the world, but I do know there can be a revival in you!

I do know that as each of us faces the spiritual battles we have in our hearts and lives that we can know that victory is certain. The battle is there <u>for the victory</u>. Look at what the Word of God says:

> 1 Corinthians 10:13 There hath no temptation taken you but such as is common to man: but **God *is* faithful**, who will not suffer you to be tempted above that ye are able; but will with the temptation also make a way to escape, that ye may be able to bear *it.*

God is still faithful! The tempter still does not have the opportunity to tempt us above what we are able, the temptations we have are still the same lusts common to all men, YOU ARE able to bear it, and there IS a way to escape! It is not because you will have to be a super Christian or have some mighty power only given in prophet like fashion to a few, but because we are not depending upon the faithfulness of men, but of God. God is still faithful! He will hear your prayers and He still loves and cares for you. You are saved by the same blood all believers are and filled with the same Holy Spirit. Yes, there is a battle and you are in it. However, God is in it with you.

THE ROAD TO VICTORY

Although the battle is for the victory, there are many who will never see victory. But, this is not because of some failure on God's part. God is not responsible for the decisions of some to reject the authority of His Word and the conviction of the Holy Spirit. If lost, you might find someone who knows exactly where you need to go and is willing to patiently share with you the complete plan of how to get where you want to go. The instructions may be great, but they are only "great" to you if you follow them.

The most essential part of victory is faith.

> 1 John 5:4 For whatsoever is born of God overcometh the world: and this is the **victory** that overcometh the world, *even* our **faith**.

Because the battle of victory will not be fought in our own power, we must have faith, if we are to be victorious, in God's power.

> 2 Corinthians 10:4-6 (For the **weapons** of our warfare *are* not carnal, but mighty through God to the pulling down of strong holds;) 5 Casting down imaginations, and every high thing that exalteth itself against the knowledge of God, and bringing into captivity every thought to the obedience of Christ; 6 And having in a readiness to revenge all

disobedience, when your obedience is fulfilled.

> Psalms 62:11 God hath spoken once; twice have I heard this; that **power *belongeth*** unto God.

The object of our faith is not our own ability, but God's. It is God that has the power to be faithful and make the way to bear it. When you are saying, "I can't." You are right! But, God can. In the "day of adversity" it is God that is necessary to find victory. In fact, Christians who try to fight the battle by the will of their own flesh will find themselves discouraged, defeated, and burnt-out. The one thing that hindered the ministry of the Lord on earth was a lack of faith.

> Matthew 13:58 And he did not many mighty works there because of their unbelief.

In addition to our faith, we must also have obedience. Victories are won with leadership and leaders win with a plan for victory. However, you will not be a part of the victory if you will not follow the plan.

> 2 Timothy 2:5 And if a man also strive for masteries, *yet* is he not **crowned**, except he strive lawfully.

Some like to trivialize the importance of obedience. With emotional hype they want to convince people they can be victorious while living in the enemy camp. You will not walk in your own desires and plans being disobedient to God and then somehow give Him the glory by the end result. We must have faith in God and we must have faith in God's Word.

> Psalms 119:9 BETH. Wherewithal shall a young man cleanse his way? by taking heed *thereto* according to thy word.

> Psalms 119:11 Thy word have I hid in mine heart,

> that I might not sin against thee.
>
> Psalms 119:105 NUN. Thy word *is* a lamp unto my feet, and a light unto my path.

As certain as the power belongs to God, the instruction will be found in God's Word. The road to victory is paved with your faith in God and obedience to His Word. If you can believe that God knows about the battle, believe He knows how to give the victory. I have met people who believe we have God's Word, and they understand what it teaches about sin, but somehow like to believe they are the exception to the rule. "I know what God says, but…" That is trusting in you and "you" are not the power, God is.

Because of the promises found in the Word of God we have liberty to be victorious over sin. We are not going to be victorious over sin because of who we are, but because of who God is. We are not going to be victorious because we know God has a plan, but because we are following the plan.

> 1 Corinthians 9:24-27 Know ye not that they which run in a race run all, but one receiveth the prize? So run, that ye may obtain. 25 And every man that striveth for the mastery is temperate in all things. Now they *do it* to obtain a corruptible crown; but we an incorruptible. 26 I therefore so run, not as uncertainly; so fight I, not as one that beateth the air: 27 But I keep under my body, and bring *it* into subjection: lest that by any means, when I have preached to others, I myself should be a castaway.

A person can fight with the greatest of zeal, the most earnest desire to win, the greatest support for the referees and the others involved, but if he breaks the rules he will be disqualified. Paul did not doubt victory was possible, but knew there was a plan for victory that must be followed. Sin is the opportunity for Victory. It is not the reason for compromise, doubts, or defeats. If we did not have the battle with sin, we would not have the opportunity to experience the victory over sin. Sin cannot be a partner in the battle. It can only be the defeated in order to see a victorious life for Christ.

THE COMPROMISE WITH SIN, OUR LIBERTY TO STAND

WHY DOESN'T GOD JUDGE THEM?

The scriptures prophesy that there will be a time of apostasy:

> 2 Thessalonians 2:3 Let no man deceive you by any means: for *that day shall not come,* except there come a **falling away** first, and that man of sin be revealed, the son of perdition;

According to Strong's Concordance the words "falling away" come from the Greek word "ἀποστασία" "apostasia."[4] Without any doubt whatsoever, we know the Bible clearly teaches that there will be a time when believers will turn from the truth and follow false teaching.

> 1 Timothy 4:1 Now the Spirit speaketh expressly, that in the latter times some shall depart from the faith, giving heed to seducing spirits, and doctrines of devils;

> 2 Timothy 3:13 But evil men and seducers shall wax worse and worse, deceiving, and being deceived.

> 2 Timothy 4:3-4 For the time will come when they will not endure sound doctrine; but after their own

---

[4] Strong's Greek Lexicon, Online Bible Edition, Version: 4.41, Copyright © 1992 – 2014.

> lusts shall they heap to themselves teachers, having itching ears; 4 And they shall turn away *their* ears from the truth, and shall be turned unto fables.

> 1 John 2:18 Little children, it is the last time: and as ye have heard that antichrist shall come, even now are there many antichrists; whereby we know that it is the last time.

> Jude 1:17-18 But, beloved, remember ye the words which were spoken before of the apostles of our Lord Jesus Christ; 18 How that they told you there should be mockers in the last time, who should walk after their own ungodly lusts.

It is clear that the Bible teaches there will be false teachers and apostate believers in the end times. There have always been false teachers. We read about the first one in the book of Genesis:

> Genesis 3:4-5 And the serpent said unto the woman, Ye shall not surely die: 5 For God doth know that in the day ye eat thereof, then your eyes shall be opened, and ye shall be as gods, knowing good and evil.

As soon as God had established a law, the devil sought to cast doubt upon it and even deny it! It is not a trial of our faith to see the wickedness of the devil in Genesis 3. However, when the deception hits closer to home good men will start to ask why? God doesn't just tell us there will be false teachers, but he tells us where they will come from:

> 2 Peter 2:1 But there were false prophets also among the people, even as **there shall be false teachers among you**, who privily shall bring in damnable heresies, even denying the Lord that bought them, and bring upon themselves swift destruction.

This is when we start to struggle with it. We can imagine false teaching among the cults and God deniers, but among the brethren, that can't be.

In order for the prophesies of 1 Timothy, 2 Timothy, 1 John, Jude, and 2 Peter to be fulfilled, there must be a process of falling away. False doctrine must take root in those who are "among you." There must be those people who will sneak in and counter or undermine true doctrine. There must be those who obtain an understanding of true doctrine and reject it. There must be those who practice true doctrine and turn or fall from it. It's possible that true Biblical doctrine never took sincere root in their heart, but to the outside observer it seemed to be so. Paul knew it would happen during his time and warned the church at Ephesus:

> Acts 20:29-30 For I know this, that after my departing shall grievous wolves enter in among you, not sparing the flock. 30 Also of your own selves shall men arise, speaking perverse things, to draw away disciples after them.

There will be the false teachers, and there will be those who are influenced by them. They themselves may not be teaching the heresy, or perhaps the heretical teaching may not have originated with them, but they are drawn by the siren sounds of success or popularity. They are lured into weakness by the desire to please all and they have for their example those who seem to have great success, wealth, and fame while living for their lusts and praising Jesus! 2 Timothy 4:3 teaches us that people, "*…will not endure sound doctrine; but after their own lusts shall they heap to themselves teachers, having itching ears…*"

We lust for things that are pleasing to the flesh. The motivation for people not to stand on sound doctrine will be lust. We may imagine that lust is only associated with immorality, but we may lust for wealth, influence, and popularity. In the ministry this may manifest itself in a desire to have a greater following, community influence, and a financially stable ministry. Someone struggling with their lot in life may think they would never compromise their convictions, but when they are looking for a shortcut to success they are seduced by the draw of rewards. They don't want to "fight the fight." They want be a pleaser of people. The path of the least resistance is the easiest to follow.

Some will teach false doctrine, some will allow it. There are those who will covet the things of this world and change their doctrine and convictions and there are those who will, "fight the good fight of faith." They will watch as others give in to pressures of popularity while they are rejected for their convictions. The fight is long and hard and they begin to see those who are not taking the stand as a kind of cheater. Cheating is not right and it's not fair. They pain in their heart at the sight of apostasy and wonder, "why doesn't God judge them!" There is the battle. Without the battle there will be no victory. As certain as there are some who will yield to the pressure of not enduring sound doctrine, there are others who will not yield and will endure. This is to the glory of God. God told us we would have false doctrine in the end of the world, but He also told us we would have truth!

> 1 Peter 1:25 But the word of the Lord endureth for ever. And this is the word which by the gospel is preached unto you.

ENDURE!

2 Timothy 4:3 tells us some, "*will not endure sound doctrine…*" and 1 Peter tells us the Word of the Lord will! The word, "endure" by application means there will be adversity. You will not have endurance when there is no effort, challenge, or adversity. Endurance is a brave and courageous thing, but it requires opposition to manifest itself.

Webster's 1828 dictionary gives these definitions for endure[5]:

> **ENDU'RE**, v.t. [L. durus, duro.]
> 1. To last; to continue in the same state without perishing; to remain; to abide.
> The Lord shall endure forever. Psa 9.
> He shall hold it [his house] fast, but it shall not endure. Job 8.
> 2. To bear; to brook; to suffer without resistance, or without yielding.
> How can I endure to see the evil that shall come to my people? Est 8.
> Can thy heart endure, or thy hands be strong? Ezek 22.
>
> **ENDU'RE**, v.t. To bear; to sustain; to support without breaking or yielding to force or pressure. Metals endure a

---

[5] Webster's 1828 Dictionary, e-Sword version 10.2.0, Copyright © 2000 – 2013.

> certain degree of heat without melting.
> Both were of shining steel, and wrought so pure.
> As might the strokes of two such arms endure.
> 1. To bear with patience; to bear without opposition or sinking under the pressure.
> Therefore, I endure all things for the elect's sake. 2 Tim 2.
> If ye endure chastening, God dealeth with you as with sons. Heb 12.
> 2. To undergo; to sustain.
> I wish to die, yet dare not death endure.

If God removed adversity, he would remove endurance. In Jr. High I ran cross country. During one of our races I was side-lined because of an ankle injury. I still attended the meet and stood beside the coach and watched the runners finish. I remember one guy racing across the finish line – not in first place. I exclaimed to the coach, "wow, look at that guy go!" I was impressed with anyone having the energy to cross at that speed. The coach told me, "If he really made an effort, he would not be able to sprint across the line." I realized at that moment that what would have impressed our coach was not a flashy finish, but endurance, giving it all you got, spending every ounce, and pushing yourself to the last. In this case, he may have crawled across the finish in first place.

Have you ever tried to estimate the success of a lone runner? The best you could do is time them and compare it to a known result or time. However, you might not be comparing a run under the same conditions. Competition manifests the struggle and the effort that it takes to win. Imagine an Olympic event with one and only one athlete. You might be able to use the word "athlete" but not "competitor." It takes adversity to win the prize.

Paul wrote to the Corinthian church,

> 1 Corinthians 9:24-26 Know ye not that they which run in a race run all, but one receiveth the prize? So run, that ye may obtain. 25 And every man that striveth for the mastery is temperate in all things. Now they *do it* to obtain a corruptible crown; but we an incorruptible. 26 I therefore so

> run, not as uncertainly; so fight I, not as one that beateth the air:

We are in a spiritual battle and what glorifies the Lord is our defeat of the adversary. The abiding effort in our struggle demonstrates our endurance by faith. Endurance is an important part of the essential elements of character, our service to God, and God's work. 1 Peter tells us God's Word will endure; Romans 9 that God will endure; 1 Corinthians 13 that love will endure; and in Hebrews 12 we see the endurance of the Lord:

> Hebrews 12:2 Looking unto Jesus the author and finisher of *our* faith; who for the joy that was set before him **endured** the cross, despising the shame, and is set down at the right hand of the throne of God.

God promises the believer that endures blessings:

> James 1:12 Blessed *is* the man that **endureth** temptation: for when he is tried, he shall receive the crown of life, which the Lord hath promised to them that love him.

The real question is not, "why do we have adversity?" but, "will you endure?" We want to be blessed by God, but we want to have the prayer of Jabez, but not the endurance of James. Again, the endurance and the love go hand and hand. Love is demonstrated, tested and proved. Endurance is just another opportunity to show our love.

We know not all will endure and that some will. Some, "will depart," so we can be sure there will be something to depart from and that some will not depart. Some will not "endure sound doctrine." Therefore, there will be sound doctrine being taught and stood for that some will not endure. As I read 2 Timothy I believe you will be on one side or the other. You may struggle with what exactly the enduring or not enduring of sound doctrine will be, but you can be certain that there will be a struggle.

There will always be someone who will have their flashy moment in the lime light, that showy sprint at the finish line. But, then there will be those who we know had endurance. When I was in college we had the well known Dr. A. V. Henderson as a chapel speaker. He was given an introduction expounding upon his achievements and various accolade's. This was concluded with the statement, "So, I give to you, the GREAT A. V. Henderson!" We all stood with applause. When he stood behind the pulpit Brother Henderson gave this sobering response, "Never call a man great while he is still alive, because you do not know what he will do." He was right. Endurance is proven in the finish.

IT'S AN OPPORTUNITY

We see the progression we can expect concerning false doctrine in the book of 2 Timothy:

> 2 Timothy 3:1 This know also, that in the last days perilous times shall come.

> 2 Timothy 3:8 Now as Jannes and Jambres withstood Moses, so do these also resist the truth: men of corrupt minds, reprobate concerning the faith.

> 2 Timothy 3:12-13 Yea, and all that will live godly in Christ Jesus shall suffer persecution. 13 But evil men and seducers shall wax worse and worse, deceiving, and being deceived.

> 2 Timothy 3:14-17 But continue thou in the things which thou hast learned and hast been assured of, knowing of whom thou hast learned *them;* 15 And that from a child thou hast known the holy scriptures, which are able to make thee wise unto salvation through faith which is in Christ Jesus. 16 All scripture *is* given by inspiration of God, and *is* profitable for doctrine, for reproof, for correction, efor instruction in

> righteousness: 17 That the man of God may be perfect, throughly furnished unto all good works.

Paul knew that his end was near, but knowing what God's Word prophesied, he knew there would be false teachers and apostasy. Believing in the imminent return of the Lord, he knew if the Lord was not to return in his life, he may very well do so in the life of Timothy. His words to Timothy were to continue! Not just continue and press on by sheer will or determination, but continue in the Word of God. Paul wrote to the church in Thessalonica: *2 Thessalonians 2:15 "Therefore, brethren, stand fast, and hold the traditions which ye have been taught, whether by word, or our epistle."*

The account of Paul's visit to Thessalonica in the book of Acts indicates that there was a struggle over scriptural authority. He compared them in a negative light to the people of Berea:

> Acts 17:11 These were more noble than those in Thessalonica, in that they received the word with all readiness of mind, and searched the scriptures daily, whether those things were so.

To me, it seems that the believers of Thessalonica where going to have a battle. The people there did not receive the word with "readiness of mind." So, they were told to hide their convictions, ease off and try to be more acceptable to the community, be more inclusive and except the difference found in others…NOT! They were told to STAND! The weakness of some was the opportunity to show the strength of others. One man's compromise reveals another man's stand. Compromise is the opportunity to stand.

IT'S ALL ABOUT DOCTRINE

We learn, especially, from the letters that Paul wrote to Timothy and Titus that the issues that will most beset us are issues of doctrine. In the three books written to these two men he emphasized doctrine fifteen times. For emphasis of this point let me paste the word search on this subject:

> 1 Timothy 1:3 As I besought thee to abide still at Ephesus, when I went into Macedonia, that thou mightest charge some that they **teach no other doctrine,**

> 1 Timothy 1:10 For whoremongers, for them that defile themselves with mankind, for menstealers, for liars, for perjured persons, and if there be any other thing that is **contrary to sound doctrine;**

> 1 Timothy 4:6 If thou put the brethren in remembrance of these things, thou shalt be a good minister of Jesus Christ, nourished up in the words of faith and of **good doctrine,** whereunto thou hast attained.

> 1 Timothy 4:16 Take heed unto thyself, and unto **the doctrine;** continue in them: for in doing this thou shalt both save thyself, and them that hear

thee.

1 Timothy 5:17 Let the elders that rule well be counted worthy of double honour, especially they who **labour in the word and doctrine.**

1 Timothy 6:1 Let as many servants as are under the yoke count their own masters worthy of all honour, that the name of God and ***his* doctrine** be not blasphemed.

1 Timothy 6:3 If any man teach otherwise, and consent not to wholesome words, *even* the words of our Lord Jesus Christ, and to **the doctrine which is according to godliness;**

2 Timothy 3:10 But thou hast fully known **my doctrine,** manner of life, purpose, faith, longsuffering, charity, patience,

2 Timothy 3:16 All scripture *is* given by inspiration of God, and *is* **profitable for doctrine,** for reproof, for correction, for instruction in righteousness:

2 Timothy 4:2-3 Preach the word; be instant in season, out of season; reprove, rebuke, exhort with **all longsuffering and doctrine.** 3 For the time will come when they will not endure **sound doctrine;** but after their own lusts shall they heap to themselves teachers, having itching ears;

Titus 1:9 Holding fast the faithful word as he hath been taught, that he may be able **by sound doctrine both to exhort and to convince the gainsayers.**

Titus 2:1 But speak thou **the things which**

> **become sound doctrine:**
>
> Titus 2:7 In all things shewing thyself a pattern of good works: **in doctrine *shewing* uncorruptness,** gravity, sincerity,
>
> Titus 2:10 Not purloining, but shewing all good fidelity; **that they may adorn the doctrine of God our Saviour in all things.**

This may seem verbose, and you may wonder why I listed each of the verses. I can tell you simply, because as clear as it is in these letters written to pastors that doctrine is the paramount, there are many pastors today who believe it is minor.

In Paul's inspired letters to these two pastors doctrine is important! According to Strong's Concordance the word "doctrine" used in these verses comes from the Greek word διδασκαλία – didaskalia and it simply means, "teaching or instruction."[6] What was already taught was important and what would be taught was also important. It said who you were and who you followed. It was something that identified you. You were adorned with it, you wore it. You taught it without corruption, which means some, could corrupt it. There was good doctrine and there was bad doctrine. In fact there would be some who would follow the, "doctrine of devils." Doctrine was expressed in what was preached, what was taught, and how people lived. Doctrine is important.

One may ask, "What exactly is sound doctrine?" Doctrine is something that is taught. However, we must be careful to identify sound doctrine as that which is taught by God through His Word and is consistent with a holy life and principles of scripture.

1 Timothy 1:10 says, *"For whoremongers, for them that defile themselves with mankind, for menstealers, for liars, for perjured persons, and if there be any*

---

[6] Strong's Greek Lexicon, Online Bible Edition, Version: 4.41, Copyright © 1992 – 2014.

other thing that is contrary to sound doctrine..."

In this passage we have several areas of sin that are identified as being contrary to sound doctrine. In our society today people may have an abundant of views about all these areas of morality, but Paul is not talking about what men think, he's talking about the teaching that comes from God's Word. Notice: 1 Timothy 1:8 *"But we know that the law is good, if a man use it lawfully;"* and 1 Timothy 1:11 *"According to the glorious gospel of the blessed God, which was committed to my trust."*

What makes doctrine sound is that it is founded upon an unchanging God and not the ever changing prejudices and opinions of men. It is not sound because people like it or it is most widely received. It is sound because faith in God is sound. Trust in God's Word is sound. It is not that we teach something well or better than someone else, but that, by faith, we stand on what God teaches regardless of what others think. In John 15 we have the message of how Christ is the vine and we are the branches. Christ said, *"without me ye can do nothing."* Our enduring strength comes from the Lord. John 15:8 says, *"Herein is my Father* **glorified**, *that ye bear much fruit; so shall ye be my disciples."* When we endure the trials of life we glorify the Lord. It is an opportunity for God to demonstrate His power and grace upon those who put their trust in Him. The falling away of some is an opportunity for the stand of others.

The prevailing bad witness of some will be the example to fall or the example to stand. Because some will see those who fall and seem to have success in some earthly carnal form, their temptation will be to fall away as well. Those who abide in Biblical doctrine despite adversity will set the mark of endurance. Those who yield to the will of men will fail that test. The struggle to stand on truth is an opportunity to please the Lord and win the race of sound doctrine.

"CAN TWO WALK TOGETHER, EXCEPT THEY BE AGREED?" AMOS 3:3

One of the areas we struggle with is doctrinal separation. We know there will be people who are off on doctrine. Some will have a stronger concern about influence than others. Some will be concerned about certain areas of doctrine, while others may have a broader concern with fellowshipping with those who differ in what is taught.

Clearly there are some things that should not be tolerated by believers and separation is taught in God's Word:

> Galatians 1:8 But though we, or an angel from heaven, preach any other gospel unto you than that which we have preached unto you, let him be accursed.

> 1 Corinthians 5:11-13 But now I have written unto you not to keep company, if any man that is called a brother be a fornicator, or covetous, or an idolater, or a railer, or a drunkard, or an extortioner; with such an one no not to eat. 12 For what have I to do to judge them also that are without? do not ye judge them that are within? 13 But them that are without God judgeth. Therefore put away from among yourselves that wicked person.

> 2 Thessalonians 3:14-15 And if any man obey not our word by this epistle, note that man, and have no company with him, that he may be ashamed. 15 Yet count *him* not as an enemy, but admonish *him* as a brother.

> Romans 16:17 Now I beseech you, brethren, mark them which cause divisions and offences contrary to the doctrine which ye have learned; and avoid them.

The Bible is also clear that there will be moments in our life when we as individuals will have to make a decision not to fellowship with someone else:

> Proverbs 22:24 Make no friendship with an angry man; and with a furious man thou shalt not go:

> 2 Corinthians 6:14 Be ye not unequally yoked together with unbelievers: for what fellowship hath righteousness with unrighteousness? and what communion hath light with darkness?

This separation seems to be conditioned upon the degree of relationship one will have. Don't make a "friendship" with an angry man. Don't be unequally "yoked" with unbelievers. I believe a detailed study will show that what are emphasized here are companionship and a joint effort. We are not going to avoid all angry people always, and we are certainly not going to avoid all unbelievers or else we will fail to get the gospel to the world. But, their testimony and spirit will limit our relationship. I could imagine that the angry man will not like it if you will not make a friendship, and I could also imagine the unbeliever, upon discovery of his unbelief, will not appreciate your desire not to yoke together. These are opportunities to stand or not endure sound doctrine. Enduring sound doctrine will be demonstrated when the Word of God effects our personal decisions. Doctrine is not just important to what you teach, but how you live. I have counseled people not to be unequally yoked with an unbeliever in marriage, our most important life-long yoke, but not because I don't think it is a good idea, but because it is what the Word of God teaches. This is doctrine. This is part of the doctrine concerning personal relationships and separation.

PERSONAL SEPARATION AND MINISTRY BASED OR ECCLESIASTICAL SEPARATION

When it comes to not "walking together" or separation from others because of doctrine, there will be a difference between my decision to limit my relationship with someone personally, and the need to separate from someone that may affect my ministry. You can't separate with everyone you disagree with; otherwise, you would never have the opportunity to instruct, encourage, or admonish others. You may have friends you disagree with, but you hope to help them understand sound doctrine.

If you have a difference in doctrine with someone, the main issue will be who is influencing whom? This is the question that may determine separation. Are we in the position to influence or to be influenced? Is our association with someone giving them the opportunity to influence others in my church to dissent from sound doctrine? Are we placing someone in a position of influence over others by demonstrating a measure of respect or allowing them to stand in our pulpit or before our class? We have to consider if differences are important to the setting and if they will cause an issue in the church.

We meet with people all the time who we are trying to influence with the gospel or sound doctrine. It is an essential part of the ministry, *"...reprove, rebuke, exhort with all longsuffering and doctrine."* 2 Timothy 4:2. In this case, the teacher is influencing the student. However, the teacher does not want other teachers, especially heretical ones, influencing his students. Let's look at Paul's message to the Ephesian elders:

> Acts 20:28-31 Take heed therefore unto yourselves, and to all the flock, over the which the Holy Ghost hath made you overseers, to feed the church of God, which he hath purchased with his own blood. 29 For I know this, that after my departing shall grievous wolves enter in among you, not sparing the flock. 30 Also of your own selves shall men arise, speaking perverse things, to draw away disciples after them. 31 Therefore watch…

In this passage there are two groups of people who Paul warns will cause a problem in the church. First, we have the wolves. These are men who come in with the intention of devouring the sheep. In the sense of a church congregation, they come in with the desire to turn people from the doctrine that is in the church. This will cause division and strife, but they don't care about the church. They care about the influence. They may not care if the flock wanders or strays; they take no care for the flock. In other words, they may not have another church opportunity in mind for the sheep; they just want them to leave the church/flock they are in. The wolf wants to devour the sheep. In terms of a congregation they want to totally devour their influence, loyalty, faithfulness, or some doctrinal position. In the end they would like the sheep to see their doctrine or opinion as superior. They want to prove the church or pastor is wrong, and they are right. They may never see the sheep again. They are not concerned about caring for the sheep. They may ultimately be used to do nothing but scatter the people and even destroy the church. Wolves come to devour and leave. I've always taken notice when people visited whether they were coming to be taught or to teach. Whether they came to listen or had something to say.

The second group is made up of the people who are a part of the flock and rise to a new position of influence with the desire to lead others to follow them. They may have been loyal to the church and its leadership, but now they have been devoured by some new teaching or person. It may be they came upon some new teaching via social media or an outside source, but a real concern is, are they students of the wolf? Did someone else cause a spirit of division in the church that spawned ideas of rebellion and doubt as to the doctrine being taught or respect for the pastor? Did we allow the wolf in because we were not willing to stand? Did we secretly desire the popularity or prosperity of the wolf so we turned a blind eye to the influence he may have? Acts 20:28 *"Take heed therefore unto yourselves, and to all the flock..."*

Paul did not want the elders to allow the wolves to come in and devour the sheep. He wanted them to do something about it. For sure, he wanted them to teach sound doctrine that would help the sheep identify the wolf. I think it is clear that we do not want to let false teachers influence our church. This is difficult because of the internet and social media. Wolves today have an opportunity to get into a church by every home, computer, cell phone, and tablet of each member. In these cases I believe that pastors and teachers need to teach doctrine in a way that identifies truth and reveals false teaching. It is important that we do not lift false teachers before our congregation. However, on a personal level, there are people I would fellowship with, but I would not have them in my pulpit. This is the difference between what we would call personal or ecclesiastical separation. How can we ever influence others if we do not communicate on some level? This is where it gets difficult to draw the line. Do some people keep wolves for pets? By that, do we find something pleasing in the relationship, even though there may be a danger or an influence we should be concerned about?

You may say, "I don't have a problem with having a cup of coffee with that guy, though I know we believe very different." But, if they are doing something contrary to the word of God or believing something that you know to be contrary to God's word will you say something? Have you established your doctrinal limits with them, or are you afraid to state your biblical position because you do not want to end the relationship or be put down in some manner? We may find differences in where we stand, but we should be willing to endure sound doctrine.

I've considered the following statements areas of importance that might serve as a guide to where we should draw a line.

Something that would hinder my walk or my testimony for Christ.

> Proverbs 19:27 Cease, my son, to hear the instruction *that causeth* to err from the words of knowledge.

Something that would contradict or deny the stated doctrine of my church.

> Ephesians 4:13-16 Till we all come in the unity of the faith, and of the knowledge of the Son of God, unto a perfect man, unto the measure of the stature of the fulness of Christ: 14 That we *henceforth* be no more children, tossed to and fro, and carried about with every wind of doctrine, by the sleight of men, *and* cunning craftiness, whereby they lie in wait to deceive; 15 But speaking the truth in love, may grow up into him in all things, which is the head, *even* Christ: 16 From whom the whole body fitly joined together and compacted by that which every joint supplieth, according to the effectual working in the measure of every part, maketh increase of the body unto the edifying of itself in love.

Something that would cause the teaching of the leadership to be disregarded or disparaged in some way that would ultimately lead to a fractious spirit in the church or strife and division in the church.

> Hebrews 13:7 Remember them which have the rule over you, who have spoken unto you the word of God: whose faith follow, considering the end of *their* conversation.

> 1 Thessalonians 5:12-13 And we beseech you, brethren, to know them which labour among you,

> and are over you in the Lord, and admonish you; 13 And to esteem them very highly in love for their work's sake. *And* be at peace among yourselves.

> Romans 16:17 Now I beseech you, brethren, mark them which cause divisions and offences contrary to the doctrine which ye have learned; and avoid them.

Teachers who have a design to draw people away from the church.

> Acts 20:29-30 For I know this, that after my departing shall grievous wolves enter in among you, not sparing the flock. 30 Also of your own selves shall men arise, speaking perverse things, to draw away disciples after them.

If there was no sound doctrine sin would abound in the life of believers. Some will choose not to preach or teach against sin, because it does not suite their self-serving agenda. Because there are some who will compromise with sin, we have the opportunity to stand. If there were no contradiction to sound doctrine, there would be no need to call some doctrine sound. False teaching has caused godly people to stand up and be counted as someone who respects and reveres the Word of God. If there was no challenge to sound doctrine and no burden to stand on it despite opposition, if God smote every guy that had a chance to devour your sheep, the term "endure" would be unnecessary and pointless. If someone did not compromise no one would need to stand. The compromise with sin is our liberty to stand.

THE NEED TO APPEAL TO GOD, IS OUR LIBERTY TO PRAY

PRAYER IS A GOOD THING

E. M Bounds in his book, "The Essentials of Prayer" wrote,

> "Trouble and prayer are closely related to each other. Prayer is of great value to trouble. Trouble often drives men to God in prayer, while prayer is but the voice of men in trouble. There is great value in prayer in the time of trouble. Prayer often delivers out of trouble, and still oftener gives strength to bear trouble, ministers comfort in trouble, and begets patience in the midst of trouble. Wise is he in the day of trouble who knows his true source of strength and who fails not to pray."[7]

Prayer is a good thing. However, prayer has a purpose and that purpose usually begins with a need. We don't like needs, but needs create the necessity for prayer and prayer is a good thing. E. M Bounds describes a symbiotic relationship between trouble and prayer.

Jesus went to His father in His time of trouble. In Matthew 26:36 – 39 Jesus enters the garden of Gethsemane with his disciples and prays, "O my Father, if it be possible, let this cup pass from me: nevertheless not as I will, but as thou wilt." There are many ideas

---

[7] Essentials of Prayer, E. M. Bounds, digital version: http://www.worthychristianlibrary.com/em-bounds/essentials-of-prayer/chapter-5-prayer-and-trouble/

what the "cup" Jesus spoke of was. I believe it was more than the suffering; I think it was the judgment that He was to see. Not, just the judgment of man, but the judgment that would of necessity come by God His father.

In Revelation 14 those who in verse 9, "worship the beast and his image, and receive his mark in his forehead, or in his hand…" receive a cup described in verse 10, "the wine of the wrath of God, which is poured out without mixture into the cup of his indignation…" We are saved by the wrath of God, but this comes with a great price: Romans 5:9, "Much more then, being now justified by his blood, we shall be saved from wrath through him." We are saved from wrath, but we are saved because Jesus endured wrath. It is not that the wrath did not take place; Jesus endured it. 2 Corinthians 5:21 "For he hath made him to be sin for us, who knew no sin; that we might be made the righteousness of God in him." Jesus would become what He was not, so that we could become what He is. For us this is His mercy and grace, but for Him it was his moment of trouble.

The time of trouble was prophesied centuries before the event:

> Daniel 9:25-26 Know therefore and understand, *that* from the going forth of the commandment to restore and to build Jerusalem unto the Messiah the Prince *shall be* seven weeks, and threescore and two weeks: the street shall be built again, and the wall, even in troublous times. 26 And after threescore and two weeks shall Messiah be cut off, but not for himself…

> Isaiah 53:4-5 Surely he hath borne our griefs, and carried our sorrows: yet we did esteem him stricken, smitten of God, and afflicted. 5 But he *was* wounded for our transgressions, *he was* bruised for our iniquities: the chastisement of our peace *was* upon him; and with his stripes we are healed.

> Isaiah 53:11 He shall see of the travail of his soul, *and* shall be satisfied: by his knowledge shall my

> righteous servant justify many; for he shall bear their iniquities.

Jesus had a time of trouble, and no one wants to endure trouble but trouble brings its own precious fruit when the dark night ends. Psalms 9:9, "The LORD also will be a refuge for the oppressed, a refuge in times of **trouble**." Trouble gives way to a place of refuge. A refuge is a shelter; it is a place of safety when danger or trouble comes. We love to sing about the Lord being our refuge in time of trouble, but we don't like to think about the trouble coming. Trouble causes the need for a refuge and a refuge is an intimate place of comfort and protection. A place we long for and love when we find. Psalms 27:5, *"For in the time of* ***trouble*** *he shall hide me in his pavilion: in the secret of his tabernacle shall he hide me; he shall set me up upon a rock."* Trouble brings us to the secret of His tabernacle and sets us upon the rock which cannot be moved. Where is the rock, it is "up." The rock is higher than we are and higher than we will be without it!

Trouble also brought the cry for help:

> Psalms 22:2 O my God, I cry in the daytime, but thou hearest not; and in the night season, and am not silent.

> Psalms 22:24 For he hath not despised nor abhorred the affliction of the afflicted; neither hath he hid his face from him; but when he cried unto him, he heard.

Trouble will bring prayer and prayer is a good thing. Trouble fulfills one of the needs for prayer and gives liberty for us to appeal to God. We dare not appeal to God without good reason, and trouble provides one. Without the need there would be no appeal, and our dependency on the Lord and our comfort from the Lord are a great comfort.

After Jesus prays the first time He returns to His disciples and finds them asleep: Matthew 26:40 *"And he cometh unto the disciples, and findeth them asleep, and saith unto Peter, What, could ye not watch with me one hour?"*

He leaves them, prays again a second time and returns once again to find them sleeping. Mark 14:40 *"And when he returned, he found them asleep again, (for their eyes were heavy,) neither wist they what to answer him."* In this account from Mark it seems to indicate that Jesus returned, found them sleeping, but they must have realized He came back. His return must have stirred them from their sleep. But, even though they knew He was there, they didn't know what to say. I do not think it is unusual that sometimes when we have a burden even our closest friends do not know how to respond. In this way, prayer can be the most intimate and personal moments of communication in our life.

Jesus left the disciples to go to the only one who could now hear His burden, understand, and respond. He returns to that spot he found away from the disciples, away from the crowd, away from the entire world and prays saying the "same words." Matthew 26:44. This time when He returns His response to the sleeping disciples seems to change,

> Mark 14:41 And he cometh the third time, and saith unto them, Sleep on now, and take *your* rest: it is enough, the hour is come; behold, the Son of man is betrayed into the hands of sinners.

You can rest, I'm done. In this passage there are many things to observe and consider, but I would share a few ideas from this event. Jesus was not afraid to return to God and repeat the same words when they were words the poured out from His heart. Also, He prayed until He found peace. I know, people often look at this and see that He concludes that the time was coming when Judas the soldiers would appear and for that He would need to stop. But, if we look at the next verse in Mark, verse 42, "Rise up, let us go; lo, he that betrayeth me is at hand." We realize that in verse 41 He said rest and verse 42 He said rise. There was some period of time between these two. It may have been minutes, it may have been a few hours, we don't know. However, He prayed three times and on the third time, He found peace and rested.

This peace was so settled in His mind it became conviction: John 18:11, *"Then said Jesus unto Peter, Put up thy sword into the sheath: the cup which my Father hath given me, shall I not drink it?"* There is quite a difference between the first time He prayed and the statement made in John 18:11. How did this come to be? – Trouble, prayer, trouble, prayer, trouble, prayer, peace…conviction. Trouble brought prayer and prayer is a good thing.

PRAYER IS PART OF GOD'S PLAN

I've heard it said that prayer is talking to God. I understand that in essence this is exactly what happens, but prayer is more than just talking. It is not just something we do on a whim or when we are inclined by our burdens. Prayer is actually part of God's plan. By this I mean, there are times when prayer causes the work of God to be done in such a way that without prayer God's goal and plan might not be accomplished.

The first time we see prayer used for the cause of intervention is in Genesis 20. In this passage Abraham travels to Gerar to the kingdom of Abimelech. Abraham, because he feared for his safety, tells Abimelech that Sara is his sister. Abimelech takes Sara intending to keep her for himself. God came to Abimelech in a dream and they have a conversation:

> *God: "Behold, thou art but a dead man…"*
> *Abimelech: "Lord, wilt thou slay also a righteous nation?"*
> *God: "Yea, I know that thou didst this in the integrity of thy heart; for I also withheld thee from sinning against me…"*

Abimelech and God are talking to each other. Their conversation is recorded for time and eternity in Genesis chapter 20. What is interesting is what God says to him in verse 7: *"Now therefore restore the man his wife; for he is a prophet, and* **he shall pray for thee***…"* God, in His conversation with Abimelech tells him to have Abraham pray for him. Prayer is more than just telling God what we want him to know, or what we may think we need to bring to his attention. It is part of God's plan. It is how God works. God didn't just want someone to pray, he was willing to respond to Abraham's intercessory prayer for Abimelech. Part of God's plan is that God's people pray for others.

We have a similar occurrence in the book of Job. We know that Job's friends were no comfort to him during his time of sorrow and affliction. In fact, they clearly added insult to injury. Though that phrase is not in the book of Job, it's what comes to my mind when I hear it. At the end of the book God takes the opportunity to instruct and rebuke all the parties involved. He tells Job's friends in Job 42:8,

> Job 42:8 Therefore take unto you now seven bullocks and seven rams, and go to my servant Job, and offer up for yourselves a burnt offering; and my servant Job shall **pray** for you: for him will I accept…

Once again, God was speaking to Job's friends. They already knew God's opinion and command concerning the matter, but God still required the prayer of Job. In fact, God would also use prayer as a catalyst to bring blessing and victory to Job: Job 42:10 *"And the LORD turned the captivity of Job, when he* ***prayed*** *for his friends: also the LORD gave Job twice as much as he had before."* God turned his captivity when he prayed for his friends. God fully planned to turn the captivity of Job. It was His plan and presentation to the devil that Job would be victorious. He knew He would be glorified in Job's ultimate humility and obedience. But, the whole plan hinged on the prayer that came before the captivity was turned. Could it be God is waiting for us to pray for someone in order to pour out His blessings?

I have heard people trivialize the need and opportunity to pray with sayings like, "God knows my heart…" Of course God knows your heart! He knew the devil's: Isaiah 14:12 *"How art thou fallen from heaven, O Lucifer… 13 For thou hast said in thine heart…"* He knows it like He knows perdition itself: Proverbs 15:11 *"Hell and destruction are before the LORD: how much more then the hearts of the children of men?"* God

knowing your heart is not a reason to not pray, it is a reason to rejoice in the liberty we have to pray!
The heart God knew above all others was that of the Lord Jesus Christ. Notice what Jesus said to Peter:

> Luke 22:31-32 And the Lord said, Simon, Simon, behold, Satan hath desired *to have* you, that he may sift *you* as wheat: 32 But I have prayed for thee, that thy faith fail not: and when thou art converted, strengthen thy brethren.

Jesus knew that the devil wanted to destroy the life of Peter. He wanted to toss it to the wind and let it fly like chaos in the air. So what did He do? Did he say something like, "But I know God loves you anyway…" or "well, it must be His will!" Did He soundly take a defensive posture and rebuke the foe? No, He prayed for him. He knew what God wanted. God knew what He wanted. God knew what He wanted when He allowed the devil to make the design to foil the plot of God and hinder the life of Peter. Yet, Jesus prayed. Prayer is part of the plan of God. It is something God uses to work his mighty power upon the lives of men.

There are several things the disciples were encouraged to pray about. Not the least of which is the very work of God that He commissions us to do in this world:

> Matthew 9:37-38 Then saith he unto his disciples, The harvest truly *is* plenteous, but the labourers *are* few; 38 Pray ye therefore the Lord of the harvest, that he will send forth labourers into his harvest.

I've always been amazed by this passage. Whose harvest is it? God's. Whose labourers are they? God's. So it is His harvest and His workers, but He tells us to pray that He will send them to the field. Jesus suffered and died to pay the debt for the harvest. He died and saved the workers who do the work at His command. I know that God knows this and wants this to take place, but He adds the command to pray. Prayer is part of the plan of God. It is not just us talking to God when we like, and it is not just us going to Him for what we want. It is the way God allows us to entreat Him so that His mighty power can work among men. It is the world of infinite power and possibilities being bridged to the world of our needs. One must open the way with prayer because it is God's plan.

PRAYER BRINGS GLORY TO GOD

Prayer is one of the moments in life when we absolutely have an opportunity to demonstrate our faith in God. We can talk to someone and we will see the response. We may actually change our tone or even our story before the response of the listener. But prayer is us talking to God, who we do not see, as if we do see Him. It is a pure act of faith and it brings glory to God when we walk by faith. 1 Peter 1:8, *"Whom having not seen, ye love; in whom, though now ye see him not, yet believing, ye rejoice with joy unspeakable and full of glory..."* Putting our faith to practice, believing God's Word and living it in our lives glorifies the Lord. 1

God does not just want us to pray to give us something to do. He uses it to His glory. Paul did not encourage people to pray just to sound religious and pious. He, like Christ, believed in prayer and in the power of prayer. He encouraged prayer because prayer works.

2 Thessalonians 3:1 *"Finally, brethren, pray for us, that the word of the Lord may have free course, and be glorified, even as it is with you..."* Paul was an amazing Christian. He was an example to follow. But, he still wanted believers who were being taught and growing in the Lord to pray for him. God's Word is designed to be preached throughout the world and is given to the pastor that he might be *"furnished unto all good works..."* (2 Timothy 3:17.) God's Word is glorified when it does its work in the world and that work is accomplished by the power of prayer. Prayer gets its power from God, because it is God's plan, and God's design to accomplish His work. As God has chosen

it, we should take every opportunity to do it and do it without doubt or reservation. Hebrews 4:16 *"Let us therefore come boldly unto the throne of grace, that we may obtain mercy, and find grace to help in time of need."*

God loves our prayers. He cherishes them and they bring a sweet smell to His glorious presence. In Revelation 4 & 5 we have an amazing sight. Men come before the throne of God. Angels are singing praise, the victorious Lamb is worthy, heaven breaks out in praise, and the elders fall on their faces before God. In this amazing seen what is it that is carried before His holy presence?

> Revelation 5:8 And when he had taken the book, the four beasts and four *and* twenty elders fell down before the Lamb, having every one of them harps, and golden vials full of odours, which are **the prayers of saints.**

The prayers of God's people are a blessing and sweet odour to Him. Imagine that at this moment of celebration we could have a part by taking the opportunity to pray. We need to pray. The troubled time in which we live beckons our prayers. Our need to appeal to God to do his mighty work in this world is not a burden. It is a liberty; a liberty to have an intimate relationship with God like no other; a liberty to glorify the Lord and walk by faith; a liberty to appeal to His throne to have His will and power upon the world in which we live.

THE WORD OF GOD, THE PERFECT LAW OF LIBERTY

WHAT WILL YOU DO?

> James 1:22-25 But be ye doers of the word, and not hearers only, deceiving your own selves. 23 For if any be a hearer of the word, and not a doer, he is like unto a man beholding his natural face in a glass: 24 For he beholdeth himself, and goeth his way, and straightway forgetteth what manner of man he was. 25 But whoso looketh into the perfect law of liberty, and continueth *therein,* he being not a forgetful hearer, but a doer of the work, this man shall be blessed in his deed.

When I began this text I addressed the trial we may have in understanding why things are allowed to take place or why God allows people to do the things they do. One of the greatest concerns about giving attention to the deeds of others is that we may try to emulate them. In other words, we may determine to "fight fire with fire." "If people will be like this and can be like this, then wait till they see what I can do with that liberty!" We may also, because of covetousness or lust, try to imitate them. We are selfish by nature. We think about ourselves and give more attention to our own wants than anyone else around us. In our age they have created the selfie-stick. So now we can take pictures of ourselves in such a position that it actually looks like someone would take the time to do it.

However, we do not need anyone else, do we? This issue is addressed in many Bible passages. So, when we see someone else feeding the desire of their flesh, although we may be initially repulsed by this, that repulsion can quickly lead to envy, entitlement, and then jealousy.

In the early days of coming to Hungary one of the most trying moments was going to police headquarters to apply for your visa and long-staying permit. Today the entire process is handled by the office of Immigration and Naturalization and is done so with professionalism and, one might even say, kindness and a helpful attitude. They have come a long way in this area. When we applied for these permits in the 90's one could expect tension, stress, and even a little fear.

Generally, you entered a waiting room and sat down. The officer you needed to speak to was behind a closed door. You dare not knock on the door, because although there were no windows in the door or wall, he or she already knew you were there, knew why you were there, and knew what you wanted. Knocking on the door would be unnecessary and rude to all the others in the room. Americans hated this moment. We want to knock and every fiber in our being felt like we should. I saw someone knock, once. The captain came out and began yelling at them and asking rhetorical questions like, "do you see all these other people here? Don't you think they would like to knock? Is anyone else knocking?" It inspired me not to knock.

There was also an unspoken rule about who was next. You entered the room, looked around, and realized all these people are in front of me. Everyone else who comes in is after me. In fact, sometimes a person will come in and ask, "Who was the last to arrive?" so, they know who they were after. The door opens, the next person steps up to it, and kindly and humbly presents their case or application. One day we were sitting patiently in the waiting room, the door opened and someone jumped up out of sequence. You could feel the tension rise in the room. The Hungarian we sat next to murmured, "nagyképű!" I learned, nagy meant big and kép meant picture, but in this situation it applied to your personal picture, your face. So, it was like calling the person, "big faced!" That is what they call someone who is stuck up or bold in a rude way. We might say, "Who do they think they are?" They would just say, bigface! I can tell you right now, at that moment nobody liked Mr. Bigface.

The first response seemed to be that they hoped the captain would realize Bigface was out of line and give him a good chewing out. That was the moment of envy. "I hope she gives it to him good!" Well, that didn't happen. Bigface succeeded in his effort to rudely cut the people in front of him. It is amazing how quickly that repulsion turned to entitlement. I knew several other people were wondering if they should jump out of line next. After all, maybe this is just what we do now. Bigface wasn't rude, he was an innovator. Soon, the captain emerged and announced she was taking a lunch break, come back in an hour. When we returned there were several applicants for the Bigface position. In fact, now the response was not anger at Bigface but frustration that you didn't get to be the Bigface first! This was jealousy, "He took my Bigface position!" We quickly moved from repulsion to envy, to entitlement, and then jealousy. By the way, if you're wondering how things developed, the captain realized what was happening, emerged, scowled, all the Bigfaces sat down in unison, and we continued in order.

When we see people doing things for the motivation of their own flesh we have the temptation to want to do the same. But, God does not want us to do what we see others do. He wants us to be "doers of the Word," and if we are going to have examples to follow He wants them to be "doers of the Word." Doing the Word requires a measure of faith. You must come to the realization that the best thing for you to do is not what some might perceive as success, not even what appears to be successful at the moment, but what God says. You do this because you know that the final result of our actions will always prove that the best thing for us to do is obey God and His Word. This is the application of Hebrews 11:6: "But without faith it is impossible to please him: for he that cometh to God must believe that he is, and that he is a rewarder of them that diligently seek him." By faith, we follow the Word of God, knowing that our reward will come from God. We also recognize that God's intention is to reward us and that this can only happen when we obey. Obeying the Word of God gives God the liberty to bless us.

IT'S THE LAW

Our Bible is the "perfect LAW of liberty." The word "law" is meant here in its most common basic meaning:

LAW, n. [L. lex; from the root of lay. See lay. A law is that which is laid, set or fixed, like statute, constitution, from L. statuo.]

> 1. A rule, particularly an established or permanent rule, prescribed by the supreme power of a state to its subjects, for regulating their actions, particularly their social actions. Laws are imperative or mandatory, commanding what shall be done; prohibitory, restraining from what is to be forborn; or permissive, declaring what may be done without incurring a penalty. The laws which enjoin the duties of piety and morality, are prescribed by God and found in the Scriptures.[8]

Do not think me verbose in giving the entire definition. It is a good definition and I believe there is a complete application concerning the Word of God in the life of the believer. God gave us His Word so that we could do right, think right, and know right. We are not left to our own opinions and desires. God knows what we are to do, and more importantly what will be the outcome of our actions.
God's Word is "the perfect law of liberty" in the sense that in its

[8] Webster's 1828 Dictionary, e-Sword version 10.2.0, Copyright © 2000 – 2013.

finished form God's Word will supply every need we may have to guide us in our faith and walk with the Lord. But it is a law and it is a law that must be obeyed. By creating this law the Lord gives us the opportunity to be victorious in every area of our life. He does not tell us we might, by chance, if we're lucky, be victorious. No, God has a victory in store for us for every trial.

> 1 Corinthians 10:13 There hath no temptation taken you but such as is common to man: but **God *is* faithful**, who **will not** suffer you to be tempted above that ye are able; but will with the temptation also make a way to escape, that ye may be able to bear *it*.

> Colossians 1:13 Who **hath** delivered us from the power of darkness, and hath translated *us* into the kingdom of his dear Son:

> Romans 8:27-28 And he that searcheth the hearts knoweth what *is* the mind of the Spirit, because he maketh intercession for the saints according to *the will of* God. 28 And we know that **all things** work together for good to them that love God, to them who are the called according to *his* purpose.

> Romans 8:31-39 What shall we then say to these things? If God *be* for us, who *can be* against us? 32 He that spared not his own Son, but delivered him up for us all, how shall he not with him also freely give us **all things**? 33 Who shall lay any thing to the charge of God's elect? *It is* God that justifieth. 34 Who *is* he that condemneth? *It is* Christ that died, yea rather, that is risen again, who is even at the right hand of God, who also maketh intercession for us. 35 Who shall separate us from the love of Christ? *shall* tribulation, or distress, or persecution, or famine, or nakedness, or peril, or sword? 36 As it is written, For thy sake we are killed all the day long; we are accounted as

> sheep for the slaughter. 37 Nay, **in all these things we are more than conquerors** through him that loved us. 38 For I am persuaded, that neither death, nor life, nor angels, nor principalities, nor powers, nor things present, nor things to come, 39 Nor height, nor depth, nor any other creature, shall be able to separate us from the love of God, which is in Christ Jesus our Lord.

It is the law that we cannot be tempted above what we are able. It is the law that God will be faithful. It is the law that all things will work out according to His will, that God justifies and nothing can condemn. It is the law that nothing can separate us from His love.

Therefore, it must be the law in determining our faith, our doctrine, our practice, and our relationship with others. We cannot separate the importance of obeying the law only when it applies to our own actions.

We want to be Bigface. We saw Bigface make his bid to succeed and be first. From our perspective he seemed to be on top, he seemed to win. And, we think he liked it. However, we really do not know what happened to Bigface. It may be Bigface got a shorter permit time than you or perhaps, though it looked like he was succeeding, the captain may have put his application aside right after he left. Even life's experience will tell us eventually the Bigfaces loose. Every Bigface is a Bigface one time too many. In the presence of God the law is not what we assume happens to Bigface, but what God says happens. God is not our adversary. He is not trying to make it difficult to teach us a lesson. He's not trying to keep us from learning secrets and shortcuts that will make it easier. He wants us to have joy. 1 John 1:4 *"And these things write we unto you, that your **joy** may be full."* He wants us to have joy and He needs us to have humility. He wants us to be humble because only in humility will we accept His authority in our life and His authority is what we need. Many times I have heard that God only promises good success in one verse:

> Joshua 1:8 This book of the law shall not depart out of thy mouth; but thou shalt meditate therein

> day and night, that thou mayest observe to do according to all that is written therein: for then thou shalt make thy way prosperous, and then thou shalt have good success.

This success will be determined by whether we will put our faith in our own judgment or in God's Word. God's Word is the perfect law. It does not need to be augmented with our experiences or opinions. It does not need to be reformed to fit our current cultural practices. It does not change from place to place and from application to application. It is dependable and unmovable. We need it. We cannot let the world and those influenced by it determine our walk. We should not be doers of the world, but doers of the Word! What are you doing? Are you angry at Bigface and so acting like Bigface? You will do better to be a doer of the Word.

WHAT IS FAIR?

When we struggle with doing right and wrong sometimes the idea that might come to mind is what is fair? This seems to be an overused concept by people today. They don't want to think about what is right, because they don't believe they need to be right. So, if you are not going to be right a close substitute is for you to be fair. It may not be perfect, but it is fair. If we look at the motivation and excuses used in the fall of man as recorded in Genesis 3 the concept of what was fair was a major part. The devil presented the idea of knowing good and evil as being like gods. This might be considered to be fair, since God knows it is only fair if we do too. The same thing happened when it came to blame. It was not Adam's fault it was Eve's and God gave her to him, just to be fair. We still have the same crooked thinking today.

God's righteousness is not based on bargaining and fair trade, it is based on truth. When God judges what is fair, it is not a judgment based on two loosing parties. It is not two mutually faulty parties trying to compromise the least damage to each other. God's fairness is based on the standard of righteousness. God is holy. He has no sin and is not motivated by selfishness. What God thinks is fair for your neighbor will be fair for you, even if you do not think so. If every man were to follow God's standard of fairness there would be much fewer conflicts, in the world as well as in the church. Sacrificial love and the spirit of self-sacrifice should be distinguishing marks of spiritual leaders in our local congregation. We may judge it unfair to always give others the preference, but God does not. God does not, because God did not.

Our responsibility to God and to one another is summed up in the Scriptures:

> Luke 10:27 …Thou shalt love the Lord thy God with all thy heart, and with all thy soul, and with all thy strength, and with all thy mind; and thy neighbour as thyself.

> 1 John 3:23 And this is his commandment, That we should believe on the name of his Son Jesus Christ, and love one another, as he gave us commandment.

God's perfect law of liberty removes motives, prejudices, suspicion, and self-interest from our judgment and lets His Word guide us in a way that is anchored in truth and righteousness. It is a way to have impartial judgment that is not just fair, in the sense of comparing man's actions and motives with man's, but fair, equitable and just. One of the reasons for the Book of Proverbs is equitable judgment: *Proverbs 1:3 "To receive the instruction of wisdom, justice, and judgment, and equity…"*

EQ'UITY, n. [L. oequitas, from oequus, equal, even, level.]

> 1. Justice; right. In practice, equity is the impartial distribution of justice, or the doing that to another which the laws of God and man, and of reason, give him a right to claim. It is the treating of a person according to justice and reason.
> 2. Justice; impartiality; a just regard to right or claim; as, we must, in equity, allow this claim.[9]

God's Word has the liberty to make judgments that are based on equality for all. God demonstrates this in His actions towards man

[9] Webster's 1828 Dictionary, e-Sword version 10.2.0, Copyright © 2000 – 2013.

and teaches us to do the same.

We want God to judge equitably and He will because He is righteous He has no sinful nature or desire to influence His judgment.

> Psalms 98:8-9 Let the floods clap *their* hands: let the hills be joyful together 9 Before the LORD; for he cometh to judge the earth: with righteousness shall he judge the world, and the people with equity.

Israel was judged by God, partly, because of perverted equity.

> Micah 3:9-12 Hear this, I pray you, ye heads of the house of Jacob, and princes of the house of Israel, that abhor judgment, and pervert all equity. 10 They build up Zion with blood, and Jerusalem with iniquity. 11 The heads thereof judge for reward, and the priests thereof teach for hire, and the prophets thereof divine for money: yet will they lean upon the LORD, and say, *Is* not the LORD among us? none evil can come upon us. 12 Therefore shall Zion for your sake be plowed *as* a field, and Jerusalem shall become heaps, and the mountain of the house as the high places of the forest.

God's Word is our guide for what is right and wrong:

> Psalms 119:105 Thy word *is* a lamp unto my feet, and a light unto my path.

The person that is easiest to judge by God's Word is ourselves, our truest relationship with God comes from the heart and this is a place we only share with the Lord:

> John 4:24 God *is* a Spirit: and they that worship him must worship *him* in spirit and in truth.

We should want to treat others the way we would want to be treated, not with hypocrisy

> Matthew 7:1-5 Judge not, that ye be not judged. 2 For with what judgment ye judge, ye shall be judged: and with what measure ye mete, it shall be measured to you again. 3 And why beholdest thou the mote that is in thy brother's eye, but considerest not the beam that is in thine own eye? 4 Or how wilt thou say to thy brother, Let me pull out the mote out of thine eye; and, behold, a beam *is* in thine own eye? 5 Thou hypocrite, first cast out the beam out of thine own eye; and then shalt thou see clearly to cast out the mote out of thy brother's eye.

We should never let the influence of others change our teaching and faith in the Word of God:

> 2 Timothy 4:2-4 Preach the word; be instant in season, out of season; reprove, rebuke, exhort with all longsuffering and doctrine. 3 For the time will come when they will not endure sound doctrine; but after their own lusts shall they heap to themselves teachers, having itching ears; 4 And they shall turn away *their* ears from the truth, and shall be turned unto fables.

These are some examples of equitable, fair, or impartial judgment that are already set down in God's Word. Sometimes we follow our carnal nature and depart from the established judgment of the Word of God and become a judge ourselves. However, we must be careful to realize that judgment can open the door for criticism and judgment in return:

> Romans 2:1-3 Therefore thou art inexcusable, O man, whosoever thou art that judgest: for wherein thou judgest another, thou condemnest thyself; for thou that judgest doest the same things. 2 But we

> are sure that the judgment of God is according to truth against them which commit such things. 3 And thinkest thou this, O man, that judgest them which do such things, and doest the same, that thou shalt escape the judgment of God?

When it comes to judgment no one is held to a higher standard than the judge himself. If you judge something to be wrong, it is all the more reason, if you do the same thing, that you would be judged a wrong doer. Judgment belongs to the Lord, and rightly so, because He is the only one who can judge in righteousness:

> Psalms 96:13 Before the LORD: for he cometh, for he cometh to judge the earth: he shall judge the world with righteousness, and the people with his truth.

When it comes to what is right and wrong there is a liberty in God's perfect law.

THE LORD JESUS CHRIST, OUR LIBERTY TO KNOW TRUTH

ARE YOU FREE?

> John 8:32 And ye shall know the truth, and the truth shall make you free.

> John 8:36 If the Son therefore shall make you free, ye shall be free indeed.

Jesus is the great liberator. If there is one thing we can be certain he will do for us, it is make us free.

The essential freedom we have in Christ is our freedom from the condemnation of sin. Romans 6:22 – 23 says,

> But now being made free from sin, and become servants to God, ye have your fruit unto holiness, and the end everlasting life. 23 For the wages of sin *is* death; but the gift of God *is* eternal life through Jesus Christ our Lord.

In paying for the debt of our sin, Jesus freely offers the gift of salvation to all. The Bible tells us that the gift is not just salvation from sin at the moment, or until the time we sin again, but rather the gift is "eternal life." It could not be an eternal gift if there were any stipulations or limitations placed upon it. It can be eternal because of the satisfactory payment. The payment is a once for all payment that was paid on the cross for all sin.

You must receive the gift. A gift is not paid for, or else it is not a gift. A gift has been purchased by someone else and is offered to you. The only thing required to have the gift is to have a moment when you receive it. The moment of salvation is the moment when you receive the eternal gift of salvation that was paid for and offered by the Lord Jesus Christ.

This all sounds pretty clear, but it is amazing how many people struggle with it. I've met many people who believe they are saved, but have no testimony of receiving the gift. They know all the jargon of Christianity, but they still believe in some effort they have made, or some deed they have done has purchased their gift. If you have to pay for your relationship with God, it is not a gift, it would be a commodity. Commodities cannot be universally distributed, because not all people are willing to or able to pay that price. However, salvation is a gift; a gift that is offered to all everywhere because it has been paid for 100% by Christ.

I have met people in Baptist churches who proclaim they have always been saved. I ask them, "Tell me about your salvation, when did you get saved?" It is amazing that many start with, "Well, I've always known there was something different about me…" or "my parents have brought me to church since I was a baby…" Of course, you are not saved by what you have done, or because you are unique. You are not saved because you have good parents, nor are you saved despite having bad ones. You are only saved by the Liberator who liberated you from sin!

> John 1:12-13 But as many as received him, to them gave he power to become the sons of God, *even* to them that believe on his name: 13 Which were born, not of blood, nor of the will of the flesh, nor of the will of man, but of God.

An important part of the freedom we receive from Christ is wrapped up in that little word, "truth." The "truth shall make you free." It is true that Jesus died for our sins that we might be saved. It is true that only his blood could pay for the debt of sin. It is true that in dying for our sin he also had victory over the works of the devil, the power of darkness and death itself. It is also true that though others may be sincere in their own beliefs their sincerity will not save them. We cannot help others come to the truth of salvation by allowing them to believe a lie. It is not kind to compromise, if compromise will cause them to lose the opportunity to have eternal life. Salvation in Christ is a must:

> Acts 4:11-12 This is the stone which was set at nought of you builders, which is become the head of the corner. 12 Neither is there salvation in any other: for there is none other name under heaven given among men, whereby we must be saved.

As clear as the plan of salvation is people struggle with it and people struggle with their eternal security because their message of salvation is contaminated with their own doctrine and beliefs. Or, it is contaminated with the doctrine of men. It is not difficult to understand when you read the Word of God. The truth of salvation has been withheld from many people. It has been hidden by false teachers, fleshly desires and the blinding of Satan. It has been disguised in order to feign a relationship with God and escape conviction from the Holy Spirit. It has been replaced with a profession that rejects humility, repentance, and the glory to God that a real relationship with Christ is established upon. The acclaimed source, God's Word, is minimized while the teaching of men is maximized. What is the problem with man's sincere plan of salvation and God's? One is true and one is not.

In reference to the civil war, Abraham Lincoln said in a speech:

"The will of God prevails. In great contests each party claims to act in accordance with the will of God. Both may be, and one must be, wrong. God cannot be for and against the same thing at the same time."[10]

This is true of truth in general. Something cannot be true and false at the same time. Two opposing ideas cannot merit the same level of

---

[10] Washington, D.C. September, 1862; http://www.abrahamlincolnonline.org/lincoln/speeches/meditat.htm

veracity. Sometimes clever scorners try to pervert this truth by an obscure application. They say, "What is true for one person may not be true for everyone." There are situations where this does apply. I have an allergy to gluten. If I eat it, I will get sick. Maybe you don't have an allergy to gluten. So, it will not make you sick. There is still a very clear application here. I will get sick if I eat what I am allergic to. If you have an allergy to something it will hurt you in some way. Having such an obscure application does not expel absolute truth. People use these types of illustrations to doubt absolute truth, but it does exist and must exist. It particularly exists in the Word of God concerning salvation. Salvation in Christ is not a maybe, it is a must!

The information I am presenting in this book is based on the truth from God's Word. One of the issues we have when we have doubts is: is the truth we know really true? It is essential that we base our salvation on the truth of God's Word. It is also essential that we base our faith and practice on the truth of God's Word. If we begin to determine how we will believe and the doctrine we will have based on our own opinions our desires may win the day, but truth may not. Truth will set us free, so truth is essential.

> John 1:17 For the law was given by Moses, *but* grace and **truth** came by Jesus Christ.

Christ is our liberty to know truth!

One of the unique things about a Biblical world view is that truth is not arbitrary or subjective. We know what truth is, and more importantly, we know where it comes from. Truth came from Jesus Christ. This is eternal absolute truth. Every aspect of how Christ relates to me: how I present Him to others, and how I hope to fellowship with Him in an intimate personal way will be based on truth. If you deny truth that comes from Christ you deny truth, not a version or a kind of truth, but truth itself. Man wanting to deny the truth of Christ is what brings condemnation: John 3:19, "*And this is the condemnation, that light is come into the world, and men loved darkness rather than light, because their deeds were evil.*" God's statements in His Word concerning salvation cannot be true and false at the same time.

Christians, followers of Christ, should have a testimony of truth.

Colossians 3:9, *"Lie not one to another, seeing that ye have put off the old man with his deeds…"* If there is anyone that should be honest it is a believer in Christ who is filled with His Holy Spirit. The testimony of a believer is often referred to as our walk. Our walk is not just what we say, but the testimony of what we believe demonstrated in our whole manner of life. John told his church that what gave him joy was that he would hear that they, *"walk in truth."* 3 John 1:4. Our testimony should be that truth is a conviction. When I know someone is being deceptive I know they are not being led by the Spirit of God. There is a spirit that inspires deception, as Jesus told the Jews in John:

> John 8:44 Ye are of *your* father the devil, and the lusts of your father ye will do. He was a murderer from the beginning, and abode not in the truth, because there is no truth in him. When he speaketh a lie, he speaketh of his own: for he is a liar, and the father of it.

This is not the spirit we should follow, and it is not the testimony we should have. I find it disturbing when people intentionally try to practice the ministry with elements of deception. Not just that they are deceptive, as though they would hide something from those they know, but that deception actually becomes a part of their ministry methodology. They not only practice deception, but teach methods of deception to others. They give seminars on how to deceive conservative churches about their doctrine. They share pointers with fellow missionaries on how to deceive conservative pastors or potential supporters. This is not done in secret, it is spoken openly and encouraged as if it was blessed, if not, inspired by God. I call it "Deception Theology." It is the practice of deception in the work of God believing that deception is part of God's plan or design for the work. But God is not the author of DECEPTION He is the author of TRUTH! 1 John 2:21, *"I have not written unto you because ye know not the truth, but because ye know it, and that* ***no lie is of the truth.****"*

Do not deceive yourself or others. The Truth will set you free. People will say there are many versions of truth. There is not. There is truth and many lies. God settled the matter by bringing truth by Christ. Truth is not always what you agree with, or what you want, but it will agree with Christ. Study Christ and you will know truth. Be like Christ and you will be true. The Bible is referred to as the "word of truth." By giving us an absolute standard of truth and preserving that truth God has given every person the opportunity to know truth, and that truth came by Jesus Christ. Jesus Christ is the liberty to know truth.

OTHER PEOPLE NEED TRUTH

Truth is not some intimate personal thing you keep hidden away from others. It is what we must teach and preach. Sometimes this will not be received the way it should be. Have you ever watched one of the TV shows where a person is trying to sell something to a buyer; they call in an expert, who looks at it and discloses it's a fake? The seller hates him. Even if the evidence is overwhelming and easy to be seen, he hates that he just lost his gold mine. He doesn't want to hear it. He may make a statement like, "that guy doesn't know what he is saying." He might just scream and jump up and down! But, in the end, it's still a fake. The authentic article is the one that has value. We need to learn this in what we teach and practice in church.

> Ephesians 4:15 But **speaking the truth in love**, may grow up into him in all things, which is the head, *even* Christ:

Truth is not always received, sometimes it is rejected. However, truth must be told because of love. Do we think we love people more if we don't speak the truth, or are we selfishly motivated to have them like us at any cost? Do we think it is love if we let them follow lies or bind themselves in the bondage of sin? Love demands truth. Sometimes we speak the truth because we love others and we hope they will see that it is true. We may even pray for them to that end. Why? Because truth has enemies and the enemies have impure motives.

> Ephesians 4:14 That we *henceforth* be no more children, tossed to and fro, and carried about with every wind of doctrine, by the sleight of men, *and* cunning craftiness, whereby they lie in wait to deceive;

We do not want our fellow believers "tossed to and fro." Have you ever seen one of those four foot standing fans? It's great if you are having an outdoor meeting on a warm steamy night. When you turn it on it has a definite effect. You know it is there. If there is one thing we know about the internet when it comes to doctrine, it is like a big, jumbo, get it big as you can get, fan! It is a storm, tornado, and hurricane of false doctrine. It will have an effect on the ministry of the local church and like it or not, we will have to deal with it. People will not know what is false by pointing out everything that is false. There are too many lies to discover every attack on truth Satan has made. We need to proclaim the truth. But, not just teach the truth with our words, written or spoken, live the truth. Live a life that is pleasing to the Lord, influenced by the Spirit of God, and consistent with the Word of God. You can point out some false things successfully, but you really need to be grounded in the truth. When you know the truth, everything else is a lie. People need the truth. Live it!

It is hard for us to understand that there are people who, "*lie in wait to deceive…*" But, there are. Deception has many motivators and inspirations. One is pride. They want to come up with something new, or hard to be understood. Deceivers like to have something that they alone can explain or express; they want to have the preeminence like Diotrephes. (3 John 1:9) They want others to show them respect and that they are an authority like the Pharisees that wanted to be greeted with, "Rabbi, Rabbi." (Matthew 23:7) They are the preachers who are motivated by the praise of men. (2 Timothy 4:3) There are many reasons, but there is one thing that will expose every one of them, it is truth. We must be willing to stand by God's Word and the truth that came by Jesus Christ. It will be a temptation to succumb to the methods of the enemy, to deceive and manipulate for the sake of success. But, truth does not originate with us or our motives it comes from Christ and must be presented if we are walking in His Spirit.

Every believer must learn that in addition to the Word of God and the conviction of the Holy Spirit, God has given the ministry of the local church to teach and propagate truth in our lives. He called leaders to the task when He begun the first churches in the New Testament era, and still does so today:

> Ephesians 4:11-13 And he gave some, apostles; and some, prophets; and some, evangelists; and some, pastors and teachers; 12 For the perfecting of the saints, for the work of the ministry, for the edifying of the body of Christ: 13 Till we all come in the unity of the faith, and of the knowledge of the Son of God, unto a perfect man, unto the measure of the stature of the fulness of Christ:

Truth is not a hindrance to the local ministry it is a unifying factor. If there are enemies lying in wait to deceive, this is where they will try to bring division, because this is where God brings the unity that will dispel false teaching. It is not just the truth taught in church that is undermined, it is the plan of God. It is people trying to remove authority and truth and replace it with something else that is more appetizing, popularity. Don't be deceived, and don't be a deceiver. Be a unifier. Learn the truth, teach the truth, preach the truth, and stay faithful to the truth because people need truth. 3 John 1:8, *"We therefore ought to receive such, that we might be* ***fellowhelpers to the truth."*** Help the truth, don't hinder it.

AGAINST THE TRUTH?

When we talk about the people who are false teachers, or teachers motivated by self-interest, rather than the truth of God's Word; we can put them into the category of those who *"resist the truth."* 2 Timothy 3:8. We should not resist the truth, but teach and proclaim it. However, resistance is not the only way we can hinder the work of truth. James 3:14 says, *"But if ye have bitter envying and strife in your hearts, glory not, and lie not* ***against the truth****."* James is addressing the person who is deceiving themselves. Note he is talking about what takes place, *"in your heart."* We may try to project a good truthful person outwardly, but who we are is in essence of our inner man. Only the Lord knows the heart of *"all the children of men…"* (1 Kings 8:39) But, you know the bitter thoughts and feelings you have towards others. You may try to justify them, but like a knot in your belly that no one else can see, you know they are there.

What or how are you lying? Jesus said in John 14:6 that He is, "the truth." If Christ dwells in us and we fill our heart with bitterness and strife, we are not walking in His Spirit. Christ is not in control of our inner man. We may want people to believe we are walking with Him, but we are walking in the flesh. We need to be honest about this and not lie against the truth. Two opposites can't be true at the same time. Deal with the bitterness of your heart. You must be willing to forgive others. Forgiveness is not restoration. Restoration is based on repentance and communication. But, forgiveness is not based on the actions of others it is based on the example of Christ.

> Ephesians 4:32 And be ye kind one to another, tenderhearted, forgiving one another, even as God for Christ's sake hath forgiven you.

Begin with this area, which is probably the most common issue among people, but continue in other ways to be honest and true to the Lord. If Jesus is the liberty to know truth, anything we may do contrary to the truth will be contrary to work and our fellowship with the Lord.

LOVE THE TRUTH

As previously mentioned, Jesus said that He is, "the truth." John 14:6. There have been many things done against the truth, but one thing is certain. We should love the truth. The truth has set us free. (John 8:32). We should not only evaluate our relationship with others as a measure of heart right with God, but we also need to honestly look at our relationship with the Lord. Here are three questions I would suggest we could ask that reveal our love for God:

Do we communicate to God?

There have been many people in my life who I would say I love. I've had and have close friends and family that I love and pray for. I've never known someone that I love, but never communicate to or even avoid communication with. Jesus is the truth, do we talk to Him?

> John 16:23-27 … Verily, verily, I say unto you, Whatsoever ye shall ask the Father in my name, he will give *it* you. 24 Hitherto have ye asked nothing in my name: ask, and ye shall receive, that your joy may be full. 25 These things have I spoken unto you in proverbs: but the time cometh, when I shall no more speak unto you in proverbs, but I shall shew you plainly of the Father. 26 At that day ye shall ask in my name: and I say not unto you, that I will pray the Father for you: 27 For the Father

> himself loveth you, **because ye have loved me**, and have believed that I came out from God.

Prayer demonstrates our love for the Lord. Prayer is a one true act of faith on our part. In prayer we communicate to God, believing by faith that He hears us; and we pray in the name of the Lord Jesus Christ, knowing who He is. If you love the Lord you must talk to Him.

Are we obedient to God?

In John 15:10 Jesus says,

> If ye keep my commandments, ye shall abide in my love; even as I have kept my Father's commandments, and abide in his love.

Our love for God is demonstrated by our obedience. What often tries our hearts are the actions of men. We see people do things and we wonder why or why it is allowed. I wrote about the love that our relationship with God is based on and how that because of love we must have volition, the freedom to choose. Here, I say, choose love. Love the Lord.

God is not standing over your head with a stick ready to give you a good smack as soon as you wrong Him or His commandments, but He is aware of our obedience or disobedience. Obeying God's Word is an act of love. When we see the reward of obedience at the Judgment seat of Christ, I think we will be glad that we did obey Him. But, that is something yet to come and may even be difficult to imagine in such a way that it really influences our day to day activity. However, today you can choose to love God. When you know what the Word of God says, and you know what your flesh wants, you can decide to choose God. Our love for God will be demonstrated in obedience.

Are you Christ's?

> Galatians 5:24-25 And they that are Christ's have

> crucified the flesh with the affections and lusts. 25 If we live in the Spirit, let us also walk in the Spirit.

This is an interesting statement to me, "they that are Christ's." Let's examine for a moment what this could mean. We know that we are not saved by our good deeds, our works:

> Titus 3:5 **Not by works** of righteousness which we have done, but according to his mercy he saved us, by the washing of regeneration, and renewing of the Holy Ghost;

> Ephesians 2:8-9 For by grace are ye saved through faith; and that not of yourselves: *it is* the gift of God: 9 **Not of works**, lest any man should boast.

If Galatians 5:24 was saying that we are only saved if we are righteous, or if we deny the flesh and live righteously, this would contradict the work of salvation being solely done by Christ. It's interesting; on occasion I've met people who believe that our works play a part in salvation. I've taken the opportunity to show them Ephesians 2:9 to which they reply, "Oh, I would never boast…" But, the Bible doesn't teach that we are saved by works and because WE are righteous, and humble, we would never boast. It says, "lest any man should boast." That word "lest" means that we would not even have the opportunity to boast. We will have no opportunity to boast because the work is done completely by Jesus. Galatians 5:24 is not promoting a works salvation.

The Bible also tells me in John 1:12,

> But as many as received him, to them gave he power to become the sons of God, *even* to them that believe on his name:

So, I received the Lord when I believed. We are talking about the moment that I put my faith in Him for salvation. I received Him. So, Christ is mine. He is my Saviour, my redeemer, my friend, my

God, my Judge, and is coming back for me. I could write several more chapters on what I receive in Christ. His being mine is not based at all on what I have done, but on believing what He has done for me. Romans 6:23, *"For the wages of sin is death; but the gift of God is eternal life through Jesus Christ our Lord."* When I received Christ, I received the payment for my sins and the gift of God. That gift is eternal life. It was eternal life the moment I received it. It was not the possibility of eternal life, it was life itself. I do not have to worry about earning the gift, or keeping the gift. Imagine someone telling you something is a gift, you don't have to pay for it, but I'm going to keep my eye on you to make sure you earn it afterwards. But, it's a gift. No, that's still your works determining your relationship with God, not His. Galatians 5:24 is not teaching that you will lose your salvation if you do not live a righteous life. When it comes to the glory for the work of redemption there is only one person through time and eternity that will receive it:

> Philippians 2:8-11 And being found in fashion as a man, he humbled himself, and became obedient unto death, even the death of the cross. 9 Wherefore God also hath highly exalted him, and given him a name which is above every name: 10 That at the name of Jesus every knee should bow, of *things* in heaven, and *things* in earth, and *things* under the earth; 11 And *that* every tongue should confess that Jesus Christ *is* Lord, to the glory of God the Father.

This will not be like the Olympics with a Gold, Silver, and Bronze medal winners. The pedestal of honor, the glory of exaltation will belong to Christ and Christ alone.

Galatians 5:24 is talking about surrender. It refers to the person who has chosen to the Love the Lord in prayer, in obedience, and in Holy living. You are not yours; you are not the worlds, or the devil's play thing. You are Christ's. You have yielded yourself to Him in love. He will not force the relationship. He will not demand your love. He longs for it.

Galatians 5:25, *"If we live in the Spirit, let us also walk in the Spirit."*

Teaches us that we can be made alive by the Spirit, but decide not to *"walk in the Spirit."* Walking in the Spirit is not what the Spirit is doing in you, in the privacy of your thoughts and heart. It is what the Spirit is doing to you that everyone else sees. I like to think about our walk in this way: we sit down and read the Word or hear the Word taught or preached in church. It influences us. It touches our hearts. God's Holy Spirit convicts us about what we do and don't do. Perhaps, we respond at an altar call or pray with a fellow believer. Perhaps we bow our head and confess our sins to God. But, at that moment God's Holy Spirit is working on us. Now, we get up and leave. Do we carry the decision with us? Do others see the change in our countenance, actions, or words? The testimony that is affected by the Spirit of God is our walk in the Spirit. When we crucify the flesh, we have the liberty to walk in the Lord!

VICTORY IN CHRIST

You cannot have a victory without a battle. All the conflicts we have in this world are opportunities for us to yield ourselves to God. They are moments of conflict where we decide to follow Christ or not, to put our faith in God or not. They are not opportunities to lose, they are opportunities to win.

The Bible teaches that because of the deeds of the flesh the wrath of God has come upon men:

> Colossians 3:5-7 Mortify therefore your members which are upon the earth; fornication, uncleanness, inordinate affection, evil concupiscence, and covetousness, which is idolatry: 6 For which things' sake the wrath of God cometh on the children of disobedience: 7 In the which ye also walked some time, when ye lived in them.

When we think about the wrath of God we probably think about hell. This is the place where God's forgiveness is no longer available. But, why did God create hell? Matthew 25:41 says, "*...Depart from me, ye cursed, into everlasting fire, prepared for the devil and his angels...*" Hell was created for the devil and the angels that followed him. It is a place of judgment and eternal separation from God. It was not created for men. Though, men who reject God will go there, John 3:36, "*He that believeth on the Son hath everlasting life: and he that believeth* *not the Son shall not see life; but the wrath of God abideth on him."* Hell is the place of separation from God and if you reject Him is the place you will be.

The wrath of God comes upon the *"children of disobedience"* because they rejected God for their own fleshly desires. John 3:19, *"And this is the condemnation, that light is come into the world, and men loved darkness rather than light, because their deeds were evil."* They refused the love of God because of evil deeds. These deeds have stolen their heart. The result of what they get is more than they bargained for. At the moment they see what they want, but they refuse to see where it leads. Many would be happy to change that decision after they are in the presence of God, but it will be too late.

What has your heart? Although, if you have put your faith in God you are saved forever, on a day to day basis you will decide to love God or love you. You decide to put on Christ and put off the flesh or you just decide to walk in the flesh. If you put on Christ this is only because Christ is yours to put on. You do not decide this in your own strength. You have this liberty because Christ has paid for it. You did not earn it, it is offered to you. Colossians 3:10 gives the alternative to living after the deeds of the flesh, *"And have put on the new man, which is renewed in knowledge after the image of him that created him…"* The new man, the opportunity for you to live for God is created by Christ. Here is where we have the strength to live for Him:

> Colossians 3:12-15 Put on therefore, as the elect of God, holy and beloved, bowels of mercies, kindness, humbleness of mind, meekness, longsuffering; 13 Forbearing one another, and forgiving one another, if any man have a quarrel against any: even as Christ forgave you, so also *do* ye. 14 And above all these things *put on* charity, which is the bond of perfectness. 15 And let the peace of God rule in your hearts, to the which also ye are called in one body; and be ye thankful.

If we put on Christ we will be thankful. We will be thankful to Him for the liberty to live for Him. God gives us the liberty to live for ourselves, to reject Him, receive Him, hate Him, or love Him. He gave us the liberty to experience everything evil and to be defeated by the enemy. But, He also gives us the opportunity to have every victory in Christ. Without the liberty to lose there would be no liberty to win. The Liberty to choose who you will serve and who you will love is the liberty that brings victory in Christ. Because only in Christ can you have victory.

www.ingramcontent.com/pod-product-compliance
Lightning Source LLC
LaVergne TN
LVHW020639100826
845148LV00012B/2242